# INNOVATING FOR
# WELLNESS

# INNOVATING FOR WELLNESS

## BRIDGING THE GAP BETWEEN HEALTH SYSTEM AND PATIENT

BY ROBERT
L. LONGYEAR III

NEW DEGREE PRESS

COPYRIGHT © 2020 BY ROBERT L. LONGYEAR III

INNOVATING FOR WELLNESS
*Bridging the Gap between Health System and Patient*

ISBN     978-1-64137-571-9  *Paperback*
            978-1-64137-572-6  *Kindle Ebook*
            978-1-64137-573-3  *Ebook*

*For my Mom,*
*always in pursuit of better*

# CONTENTS

———

# ACKNOWLEDGMENTS

———

This book would not have been possible without many people.

First always, I would not be here and this book would not have been written without my mom. Despite the circumstance, I value the lessons learned from her and our experience. I promised her I would work hard to make things better.

Next, my family i.e. my Dad, Hannah, Grandma, Grandpa, Bridget, and Aunt Viv. Thank you for your help during such a dark time and thereafter.

To my friend-family in Georgia—especially Tammy, Mark, and Charlie. Friends are often more family than family.

To Caroline, thanks for taking the MCAT and providing me with an excuse for writing this book as you studied—and for helping me develop my ideas.

To my college friends, thanks for a great time and support during the years after.

To my teachers and professors, I am always grateful for your guidance and knowledge.

To the team at New Degree Press, thanks for facilitating this process.

Thanks to the following people for their ideas, dedication to healthcare, and for your time with respect to this book:

Dr. Jerry Wilmink
Dr. Elliott Fisher
Dr. Dan Skinner
Dr. David Muhlestein
Morgan Feight
Prab Goriparthi
Taylor Justice

# PART 1

*"Innovation distinguishes between
a leader and a follower."*

– STEVE JOBS

# INTRODUCTION

———

"So, basically, you guys solved healthcare," I said with a bit of disbelief in my voice.

I said these words to Taylor Justice, a man with an incredible story. He attended West Point and was later commissioned as an Infantry officer in the US Army. Within two years of his military career, he was injured and his whole world flipped upside down. "Transitioning from the military into the civilian world was tough," Taylor reflected. "I was in survival mode at the time, but my West Point network helped me find a job at a medical device company in sales."

So, Taylor was able to find a position where he could enter the civilian world and little did he know, at that time, he was destined to co-found one of the most innovative healthcare technology companies in the country—one that is helping drive change for the costliest and deadliest issues in America.

\* \* \*

Before I ever spoke to Taylor, while I was still deep into my degree in healthcare management and policy at Georgetown University, I was looking for the next step in my life. I learned quickly and early in my college career, that, despite years of claiming that medical school was my end-goal, I no longer actually wanted to go to medical school. I knew I was deeply, and very personally, passionate about healthcare—but I was not quite sure what I wanted to do, or where I wanted to position myself in the vast industry. But, like many other students looking to continue exploring before specializing, I ended up very interested in healthcare consulting.

Before this, though, when I was looking for which area of healthcare I wanted to be in, I had sent a few applications for "fun" to a couple select start-up companies that had the potential to really flip healthcare on its head. I was batting a bit out of my league on these applications, but I figured it was worth a shot. I didn't get contacted about a job at that time, but little did I know that I would find myself not only interacting with one of those companies through this book, but leading one myself. And now, as a result, I have spent six months trying to solve some of the most challenging problems faced by healthcare today, through the use of mobile technology.

One of those companies I applied to was Unite Us—a technology company  that connects social service providers, or community-based organizations (CBOs, as they have come to be called in the health policy space) and healthcare providers through a shared platform to better coordinate and manage their services for people in need. As I began this book journey and desired to focus on technology, I knew that I needed to try and talk to someone at Unite Us. That's when I sent Taylor Justice, Co-Founder and President, a hopeful LinkedIn message trying to set-up a phone call—I got lucky and Taylor was kind enough to provide me with that opportunity.

Shortly after entering the civilian workforce, Taylor volunteered with a national veterans organization and started their local chapter in Philadelphia. The organization helped veterans and military families connect with their local communities via physical fitness and social activities. Fueled by his own experience and passion for helping his fellow military brothers and sisters, he began to notice that many veterans attending these events had several co-occurring social issues that required additional support outside of what his organization could facilitate. He realized the population was fairly "heterogeneous" despite many social programs treating the people they serve as very "homogenous" when it came to social needs. Taylor began to organize and support these individuals by connecting them to organizations he knew in the community, using an Excel spreadsheet to try and manage his workflows.

During this time, Taylor found a new job with a technology company and enrolled in the Executive MBA program at Columbia Business School. That's where he met his Co-Founder, Dan Brillman (a veteran himself), and the foundation was laid for Unite Us. Their first meeting lasted five hours—there were subsequent conversations that lasted even longer. The pair shared a knack for technology, business acumen, and a passion to connect veterans effectively to the social services they need. Seven years later (and several iterations of the platform), Unite Us is transforming the delivery of social services not only for veterans, but for all populations.

While this seems like a giant task to undertake, solutions from Unite Us are decidedly simple and intuitive. The coding, product features, and technology may be complicated, but the functionality—once you understand it—makes you hit yourself on the forehead while uttering a resounding, "Well, duh, why didn't I think of that?" As, often, the best innovations do. Not only is this true about Unite Us' product, but, like many truly innovative solutions, the actual solution to the problem is often very small, but with a huge effect.

The innovation process begins with the identification of a problem—this often comes from an individual's lived or professional experience. *This process doesn't work very well. It would be so much more efficient if this happened. What if we did it like that? I think I can do this faster and better. This is so messed up.* These are the types of thoughts that often preclude a successful innovation.

\* \* \*

What Taylor and his team did may change the face of *healthcare* moving forward—despite first operating in the sphere of social services. To better understand what happened, we first need to walk through a brief background of social services and community-based organizations in the United States.

Let us imagine, for a moment, that we are living in a small community called Smallville. In Smallville, there are people of different demographics and socioeconomic statuses. For people who are impoverished and disadvantaged, there exist organizations to help: homeless shelters, food banks, soup kitchens, job training programs, community health centers, religious aid organizations, government social service agencies, emergency departments at hospitals, etc. These organizations do wonderful things by providing services to the people that need them.

Each of these organizations operates in their respective areas, trying to be as efficient as possible so as to provide the greatest benefit to the people they are trying to help. But, the specialization of these different services is a blind spot when it comes to meeting the needs of the people they are helping. Homeless shelters provide shelter, hospitals provide healthcare, and soup kitchens provide...soup. Taylor and his team were able to see this first when they were helping veterans.

"Veterans, like the greater population, have needs that are co-occurring," Taylor said.

We typically associate "specialization" with increased efficiency. If you think back to any economics course, the idea of specialization in trade generates more benefit to each entity than if both tried to do everything themselves. If you are familiar with Jared Diamond's *Guns, Germs, and Steel*, he speaks of the importance of specialization to enable civilizations to advance from hunter-gather societies to agricultural ones that can build advanced societies.

In today's world, specialization is everything. In college, you major in something specific, in graduate school you specialize even further, in a company you see titles like VP of Human Resources, where specialization is indicated in the title. In business school, "specialization" for a product is taught through the lens of market segmentation—which defines the specific type of person or business that is the intended customer? Specialization is how the world works, but it has its drawbacks.

When looking from the individual's perspective, rather than the system's, it paints a very different picture for how individuals experience social services and the actual collection of their needs—the poorest, sickest, most in-need people are not specialized; they are diverse as a population and experience different challenges individually. Thus, they need multiple services to help them.

Taylor first recognized this phenomenon while volunteering at the veteran-support organization. An individual may be homeless, require food support, be involved in the justice system or formerly incarcerated, have multiple medical conditions, and/or be in need of job training. They may receive food from a soup kitchen, visit a food bank, see two different community health centers, and require support from a government housing agency while moving back and forth between homeless shelters. From an individual's perspective, they have a lot of required services from many different organizations. And, the person receiving the support is the only one that knows which ones they are engaging with.

The problem with the way social support organizations operate is that these individual community-based organizations may all duplicate services, perform their own additional services, and hold their own records. This is a terribly inefficient process. They have specialized, and, therefore, isolated themselves and operate along a single social need.

So, what Taylor and Unite Us did was build a technology platform that connects these organizations, but with the needs of an individual in mind and with the ability to scale the network. They built their system around both the care coordinator and the end-user. Now, using the app, the food bank knows which homeless shelter the individual stays at; the community health centers know that this individual is receiving nutritional support from the food bank; the government social services support center sees where this individual can be contacted, and also sees that the social worker from the hospital indicated that this individual has an unmet substance abuse need and can connect them to a program supported by a different local health center. This coordinated platform allows the individual's data to travel with them where they go for support. This means that processes do not need to be duplicated, an individual's needs are met, and the organizations that used to operate independently are now a part of a network that can increase their capabilities to truly help more people.

Now, the technology aspect of this process is not easy. There are thousands of lines of code, system integrations, and plenty of person-hours of work that went into building Unite Us. But, the actual solution is so simple. It solves a massive problem—that is, connecting organizations using a software system. Unite Us did not need to start its own food bank, hospital, homeless shelter, and government support agency to provide comprehensive services to the underserved in a community—an approach that is often taken to innovate on a large scale.

Unite Us simply empowered existing organizations to do what they do best. They used technology to enhance and extend the abilities of people and organizations already providing needed services. Specialization is key to create efficient, well-run organizations and to develop a deep understanding of some areas. But, often, specialization is isolating when an output needs to be more multi-faceted. An individual, after all, requires a multi-faceted approach. Humans are complex beings.

"We built out the pipes that connect everyone. We are not a silver bullet. We are a tool to connect Organization A to Organization B and keep everyone updated on the progress of the individual in need," Taylor says. During our discussion, Taylor kept mentioning that Unite Us is not anything more than a well-designed tool built by passionate, hardworking people to help the passionate and hardworking people on the front lines interacting with individuals in need. It's a small idea, but with big, amplifying effects because it solves a small, manageable problem for the end user. He did not want to claim credit for transforming a whole industry and system. He takes credit, and gives credit to his team, for building a well-designed and implemented tool that is transforming the care delivery system and industry in a way no one imagined before.

The reason that this tool drives such powerful impact—and will likely change the face of healthcare services in the US and, perhaps, globally—is that it is built to impact the well-being and health of the individual. Unite Us built a tool that addresses and solves an individual's social problems. Unite Us leverages data to **improve service delivery to people in need in an efficient way.** In any social service or health organization, the desired output that shows success is how well they affect beneficial change in individuals. Do the hospitals send patients home feeling better? Do physicians improve the health of their patients? Does the food bank put food in the hands of as many people reliably as possible? Does the homeless shelter provide a place to sleep for as many people as possible in a safe and effective manner? We measure success in terms of numbers.

*But, while often measured in aggregate, the change, or delivery of services, must occur in or to individuals.*

\* \* \*

This book is about healthcare. Specifically, the innovations and ways of innovation that are changing the way healthcare services are provided.

It goes without saying that healthcare is one of our systems that needs some serious transformation. We have all seen the news. We have seen family members get sick. We have seen our friends in the hospital. We have been sick ourselves.

Health is a ubiquitous human condition, and thus so are interactions with the healthcare system.

"In spite of all the efforts in the US to control health spending over the past 25 years, the story remains the same—the US remains the most expensive because of the prices the US pays for health services," says Gerard F. Anderson, Ph.D., a professor in the Bloomberg School's Department of Health Policy and Management at Johns Hopkins University.[1]

For those of us who work in and study the healthcare industry, we know the core problem in the system is that we pay significantly more than other countries, but we do not get better health outcomes for our higher spending. In most industries, we expect higher quality goods and services when we pay a higher price. You are willing to spend $1,000 on an iPhone versus a flip phone because the value and quality are so much higher.

In a 2003 paper written by Anderson and colleagues titled "It's The Prices Stupid: Why The US Spends So Much On Healthcare" it is made clear that disproportionate cost is a national problem.[2]

In 2019, Anderson and his colleagues wrote another paper to add additional emphasis to the discussion at hand. Its title? "It's **Still** The Prices Stupid: Why the US Spends So Much On Healthcare." The US is an outlier in terms of per capita healthcare spending (the yearly amount of spending per person in the US population), which was $9,892 in 2016. That amount was about 25 percent higher than second-place Switzerland's $7,919. It was also 108 percent higher than

1    Aspril, Joshua, and JH Bloomberg School of Public Health. "US Healthcare Spending Highest Among Developed Countries." Johns Hopkins Bloomberg School of Public Health, January 8, 2019.
2    Anderson, Gerard F, Uwe E Reinhardt, Peter S Hussey, and Varduhi Petrosyan. 2003. "It's The Prices, Stupid: Why The United States Is So Different From Other Countries." Health Affairs 22 (3): 89–105.

Canada's \$4,753, and 145 percent higher than the Organization for Economic Cooperation and Development (OECD) median of \$4,033.[3]

This has been a problem in the US for a long time and everybody has been writing the same old papers with "this year's" data for decades. The academic community, health system, politicians, and American families have heard and felt the same old story for far too long. And, truly, the prices are a part of the problem. But what often gets lost in the discussion of healthcare cost is the underlying reasons and root-causes of people needing to seek our healthcare services, regardless of what prices may be and the purpose of the healthcare system. Losing sight of these two important acknowledgments often leads people in the wrong direction when it comes to solving the problems.

People are sick and they enter the health system either looking to feel better or because they have to because their condition has declined so far that they are rushed to the hospital. **People do not seek health services for fun, save a few optional procedures. They go to the hospital because they are sick.**

The hospital and healthcare system exist because there is a demand for it due to sickness and because it provides value to our society. A physically healthier country and society is more productive, happier, and successful.

---

3   Anderson, Gerard F., Peter Hussey, and Varduhi Petrosyan. "It's Still The Prices, Stupid: Why The US Spends So Much On Healthcare, And A Tribute To Uwe Reinhardt." Health Affairs 38, no. 1 (2019): 87–95.

Frequently, only two solutions are discussed when talking about how to reduce cost in the US health system. One is to fix or pay lower prices for the same services driven by government or insurance company force and rate setting. The second is to ration care. Rationing care is denying people services as a way to reduce the utilization of finite health resources and to limit overall spending. Fixing prices, it is often argued, hurts hospitals and physicians who provide the services. Rationing care, unsurprisingly, is unappealing to our nation's citizens, and is likely not beneficial for the health of the nation—which is the point of having a healthcare system in the first place.

I like to argue that there is, in fact, a third option in solving our nation's cost and outcomes issues—one that is far more challenging and one that we do not know how to do very well on a large scale just yet, but are working on tirelessly. The things that are worth doing are often challenging. Going to the moon was not easy, but strong minds, innovation, and motivation were combined to make it happen.

Strong innovation begins with the identification of a problem and solving aggressively for that problem.

The underlying problem here lies within chronic illness or diseases that people must live with during the remainder of their lives. Diseases like diabetes, asthma, chronic obstructive pulmonary disease (COPD), congestive heart failure (CHF), heart disease, Alzheimer's disease, cancers, and other life-long afflictions fall into this category.

The important piece to understand is that these diseases often require daily maintenance by the patient through medication and lifestyle changes (diet and exercise, typically). These diseases also require more frequent visits with physicians where, in a perfect world, this is a check-in to make sure patients are self-managing their conditions well and to catch any early warning signs.

We typically have treatment solutions and the ability to manage these conditions over time provided by medical research and knowledge, but the system fails to do so in an overall effective manner. This is to say that the ways in which the health system matches the knowledge of medicine to the patient and supports the patient after that process is a major point of failure.

Seventy-five percent of US healthcare dollars are spent on chronic illness, for which we have the ability to reasonably manage in most patients.[4] But for some reason, the system fails to do so as successfully as possible.

It is when these conditions get out of control that they result in costly care episodes where an individual requires services from the emergency department, to be admitted to the hospital overnight, or to receive a high-cost procedure or treatment.

On their own, these diseases are not necessarily as costly as sudden accidents like car crashes or other catastrophic events, but they nevertheless occur frequently in the population. So frequently, in fact, that the sheer volume of individuals with these conditions is enough to drive these significant costs into trillions of dollars.

---

4    Dzau, Victor J., Mark B. McClellan, J. Michael McGinnis, Sheila P. Burke, Molly J. Coye, Angela Diaz, Thomas A. Daschle, et al. 2017. "Vital Directions for Health and Healthcare." *Jama* 317 (14): 1461.

Many of the highest-cost individuals are those with multiple co-occurring chronic illnesses, i.e. diabetes and congestive heart failure at the same time. These patients are at high risk for *very high* health service utilization because of the complexity of having and managing more than one condition at once.

These highest-cost individuals, or "super-utilizers" represent about 5 percent of the people who use healthcare resources in a year. These 5 percent of individuals represent over 50 percent of spending on healthcare services. If there were 1,000 people in a room that cost one million dollars to provide healthcare for in a year, under the 5 percent statistic, 50 of these people would be responsible for over $500,000 of the total spending. The other 950 people would the same $500,000.

The real problem needing to be solved is how the health system deals with individuals in the "chronic illness" category, or rather, how services are delivered to them. The system as it is fails to deliver effective services to these individuals in order to help support them in managing their complex chronic conditions.

Individuals with high-risk multiple chronic conditions need to be supported:

1) to maintain a positive health status, so as to manage their conditions without significant deterioration or the need for more intensive services.
2) prior to their development of these conditions, with adequate preventative measures.

Remember, at one point in their past, even our sickest people were healthy.

The focus on cost and price is important, but remember that these are real people with conditions that drive demand for these costly services. Nobody chooses to receive a cardiac bypass surgery where their sternum is cut open because it is fun. It is because they are sick, and therefore require services like this.

The truth is, the system has been trying to change prices for a long time—we know how to do that and have been trying to do that for decades—and it is the low-hanging fruit. Economists get together and decide what should happen based on their models, insurers and government change the price they pay for healthcare, and costs and prices change.

What is much, much harder is actually improving the health of people so as to remove the reason why these high prices are such a major issue. It is much harder to impact the root cause of health services-based demand.

Healthy people do not demand costly health services. No one wants to spend their time receiving health services when they can be watching baseball games, enjoying time with family, or walking in the park. Nobody wants to use their paid time off or short-term disability to receive healthcare services.

People seeking care want to feel better, but would much rather be healthy in the first place.

Improving health? Well, that's what doctors are for, isn't it? Well, yes, but doctors and their functions are a small part of the whole system, and for the purpose of this book, represent a body of knowledge and expertise that requires more effective delivery to patients.

\* \* \*

Everyone in the healthcare field talks about the cost problem, the chronic disease issue, and other big problems faced by US healthcare. Those working in this area are trying to do things like large-scale system transformation, system redesign, and national healthcare reform.

You hear politicians debate Medicare-for-All, Obamacare, and The Affordable Care Act. The latter two have been passed and implemented, yet Dr. Anderson's study in 2003 (before these national policies) and a study in 2019 are telling the same old story. We try big reform, but the discussion misses the point because we think about the problem using the same old logic and focus on driving top-down change.

Unfortunately, top-down change debated in Washington fails to take a deep look at the patients' experience with care and the ways in which patients meet the healthcare system.

This big reform often involves increasing access to health insurance as a "surrogate" for actual systemic improvement. Yes, we do know that providing access to health insurance is an effective way to improve health to some degree overall.

Access to a primary care physician and covered preventive services like flu shots is effective, but only goes so far. Once a patient has access to care, they must now contend with the healthcare delivery system, or the hospitals, physician practices, and other patient-facing organizations.

The fact is, large-scale reform is not going to solve the problems faced by front-line healthcare workers and, most importantly, the American people unless we change the way large-scale reform meets the individual.

This is where change and innovation need to occur to impact the patient. Large-scale impact sounds flashy and gets votes for politicians, and it certainly has its place, but at the end of the day, the changes that truly "move the needle" on the national healthcare situation occur at the patient level—the level of individuals. Often, these changes can come from small, simple innovations that allow for fundamental changes in the models by which the system supports patients with chronic illness.

Big healthcare movements have the potential to bring about change, but this is due to the micro-level effects that occur as a result of the environment created by these large national legislations—but micro-level innovations are the ones with the potential to drive big results because they are specifically designed for the patient. Innovations in healthcare with the potential to have a major scalable impact must be effective at improving the health of individuals.

To improve the care of individuals with chronic illness, something must change in the ways in which the healthcare system at-large interacts with the individual patient. We know that the current model of reactive, episodic, and institution-based care services does not meet the needs of patients, and thus fails to perform adequately.

In terms of movements like Medicare-for-All , if we keep on providing access to the same old system that we know is poor, then we will continue to see the same results (albeit with some small increase in overall health outcomes due to access improvements for some people who previously had no health coverage at all).

We can change prices, funding sources, insurance coverage, and big-picture things, but if the changes fail to trickle down or fundamentally alter the interaction between the system itself and a patient, the larger changes will not produce the outcome we are looking for: healthier people who demand fewer health services.

A population that is high in *wellness* is the societal goal for health.

\* \* \*

We are entering a new age of innovation in healthcare. The time and environment are finally right for these types of disruptive and fundamentally model-changing innovations to occur. In recent years, digital technology, mobile technology, and advanced analytics have become more available and widespread to enable the application of technology to the health system. But these technologies have failed to become adopted by healthcare organizations because there has been no incentive to do so.

The intersection of incentive and technology is now here. The time is ripe. New ways of paying healthcare delivery organizations have been studied, implemented, and are gaining popularity. Spearheaded by many experts and organizations—under terminologies like value-based care, pay-for-performance, and accountable care—new models are rapidly spreading across the nation.

This perfect storm is forcing delivery organizations to source, test, and adopt new technologies to extend their ability to provide and improve care to patients.

The intersection of digital health and payment model reform creates the perfect environment for patient-level innovation. This is the path forward to a better health system—one measured on its ability to maintain wellness and that has the capability to do so.

The book bridges the gap between these two innovation camps. The payment reform people are typically in health policy, economics, and traditional healthcare organizations, while digital health technology people are in start-ups, major tech companies, and some progressive healthcare organizations. The intersection between the two is a point at which innovations can fundamentally disrupt the traditional models of healthcare delivery.

This book, through stories, will illustrate how the following three topics are the path forward to driving major change in the healthcare system:

1. Fundamental Philosophical Changes
2. Payment Models
3. Digital Health Technology

\* \* \*

I first became interested in healthcare when I was very young and dreamed of becoming a physician. My dad had just had a knee reconstruction after a substantial baseball injury, obtained while sliding into home plate. A short, painful ambulance ride later, he was at the hospital and was informed he would require a knee reconstruction surgery, which was promptly scheduled and performed. Until this time, I had been pretty determined to become a firefighter, astronaut, or maybe a space-firefighter.

But during his long recovery, my dad swears that I said, "I want to be a doctor so I can take care of people like you when they get hurt and need help." I wanted to be a doctor because I wanted to truly help people. The challenge was alluring, and, honestly, who hasn't heard their parents say, "You would make a great doctor," or that they want their kid to grow up to be a doctor or a lawyer.

So, for about a decade, I followed my dream to become a physician. I asked for medical textbooks for Christmas in high school, I spent far too much time on Google Scholar reading articles, and had my sights set on top colleges.

My current view of healthcare was shaped drastically by the health-events that occurred in my family, my training as an emergency medical technician, and, later, my formal education and professional experiences in both pre-medical studies and in healthcare management and policy at Georgetown University, in Washington, DC.

During my early life and undergraduate studies, I had the tragic privilege of the best healthcare education one could receive. I was learning the academic principles of the field and then was forced to begin living the daily truth of the healthcare system when the most pivotal event in my life, to this point, occurred. My mom, who was already very sick, got about as sick as a person can get when her chronic illness began to deteriorate, and we were thrown to the mercy of the US healthcare system.

It was through this complicated, traumatic, and painful journey that the healthcare academic framework I had learned became vividly evident and unforgettable. And now, having written this book, this framework deeply informs the points and insights I make into the ways in which we, as a nation, can start to transform the healthcare system to drive the outcomes that are both needed and, truly, are the right thing to do.

One of the most evident results of this framework is the underlying presence of our humanity in our healthcare system. It's easy to think of the clinical operations, healthcare organizations, and the delivery of healthcare services as just that—operations and delivery. We speak of the system, using this terminology on a daily basis. But what occurs on a patient-level in our institutions merits our dedication to true and effective improvement efforts. At the end of the day, how we care for our nation's people is how we care for ourselves.

During our interview, I asked Taylor what he thought of as the most important aspect of his product. He said, "We built the system for the users. We have conversations with the CBOs and the people that will be using the system in their workflows. These are the people who know what they need and we give it to them."

Taylor, here, espouses one of the core tenants of "Design Thinking," or the process by which many tech companies use to develop their products—particularly products that are targeted at consumer-users. This concept is often referred to as "user obsession" or "user-centric design." Said differently, this is deeply knowing exactly what is required by your target user, so as to design your product to enhance their experience and solve fundamental problems.

When you apply design thinking to a user, system, organization, or problem, you are able to identify the small areas of improvement that can be made to take a step in the right direction toward a larger goal. Once again, Taylor and Unite Us did not have to build a large multifaceted organization to solve people's many co-occurring social, health, and economic needs—as we try to do in healthcare. They did not need to lobby for national legislation. They just needed to empower myriad organizations to work together. Unite Us harnesses the collective expertise of specialized organizations together to affect change on a larger scale. Unite Us brings together multiple, cross-sector partners to align around a common goal using their technology combined with localized community engagement. They built a tool that is becoming a small, but crucial part of a much larger impact. This impact is now rippling across different sectors and industries. Taylor and his team envision one national network, connected by technological infrastructure and supported by local team members rooted in communities.

The solution is not one technology platform to solve all of healthcare's shortcomings. But the story of Unite Us provides an example of how innovation can occur in a way that impacts patients and fundamentally changes some aspect of how a system meets its end users.

These solutions are not easy, but they are impactful. This is a new philosophy on how to think about healthcare innovation. Too often, I hear the following approaches when talking about affecting change in US healthcare. One is: "Let's bite off the whole problem and solve it." Another is: "Oh, you are living in a fantasy land thinking that you can fix this." Yet another is: "This is going to take everyone getting on the same page to fix." And, my personal favorite: "This is going to require full federal bi-partisan cooperation and sweeping legislation to fix this giant mess."

Yes, the system is gigantic—it's the largest sector of the US economy. In 2017, the sector was worth $3.5 trillion, or 17.9 percent of the national gross domestic product (GDP). Yes, there are many competing interests in the system, millions of employees, and deeply personal political angles. No, change doesn't happen overnight. But there are approaches that have been successful and will continue to be successful. They just need to be applied to the problems faced by patients in their goal of attaining and maintaining positive health and wellness.

To understand how, it is important to understand the current state of the healthcare system, how patients with chronic illness are cared for by the system, and the innovative approaches that are looking to fundamentally change the healthcare system from reactive to proactive.

# CHAPTER 1

# THE NATIONAL HEALTHCARE DISCUSSION

———

*"The president has signed the bill. I know this has confused some, but health-care reform is now law. The Senate's vote on the reconciliation fixes will modify that law, but President Obama just signed a universal health-care structure into law in the United States of America."*

This was the post written by Ezra Klein in the *Washington Post* to announce the long-debated passing of the Patient Protection and Affordable Care (aka, the ACA or Obamacare) and the subsequent signing of the bill into law by President Obama on March 23rd, 2010. Nearly a decade after this bill was passed, healthcare has gone through some major changes—many of which were driven by the ACA itself. Others, however, have come as technology has slowly improved and begun to diffuse throughout the healthcare system—a system where, historically, technology adoption has been slow (physicians still *fax* records to each other).

Similarly, the ways in which we think about our healthcare system has slowly begun to change to result in a good deal of experimentation and a rising awareness that we need to do something differently; the same old tricks are not going to cut it. The most important effect of the ACA may have been this awareness that permeated the national healthcare scene, and which brought healthcare issues into the American home. Experts were energized, the American people learned more about the healthcare crisis, and healthcare became one of the most difficult and divisive issues in politics.

The US healthcare system is broken—and has been broken—since before the ACA, and even in the years after, despite promises of major reform. If you work in healthcare, you know your own pain points and problems that perfuse your day-to-day life. If you are a human being with a pulse, you have interacted with the system in some way, shape, or form—and, most likely, you have had some bad experiences or experiences that could certainly have gone much better. These experiences made you frustrated, poorer, or, at the very least, inconvenienced. You, too, know about some of the key issues the US healthcare system faces. It certainly does not take a degree in a healthcare field to understand the challenges faced by patients. We are *all* patients.

When those of us who study the industry talk about the fundamental problem with US healthcare, it is that healthcare is too expensive and does not produce the outcomes that our nation's high spending should, and could, be producing for the people of our country. And, far too often, after a healthcare system interaction, you are left saying to yourself under your breath, "That was ridiculous."

As a reminder, the US is an outlier in terms of per capita healthcare spending, or the amount spent per person on average, which was $9,892 in 2016. That amount was about 25 percent higher than second-place Switzerland's $7,919. It was also 108 percent higher than Canada's $4,753, and 145 percent higher than the Organization for Economic Cooperation and Development (OECD) median of $4,033.[5]

Adding further fuel to the fire, according to data gathered and analyzed by the Kaiser Family Foundation (KFF)—one of the largest healthcare non-profit research organizations in the US—the US performs much, much worse than comparable countries like the United Kingdom, Canada, Germany, Japan, and Australia. The United States spends more money on healthcare per person than any of these countries, but those dollars do not produce better health comparably.

Not only are we not healthier, but our healthcare system has more medical, medication, and lab errors than other countries. *And the US has higher rates of hospital admissions for preventable conditions than these countries.* These preventable admissions are a big part of the cost problem, and are derived from our system's failure to adequately assist patients in managing chronic conditions. Specifically, conditions like

---

5   Anderson, Gerard F., Peter Hussey, and Varduhi Petrosyan. "It's Still *The Prices, Stupid: Why The US Spends So Much On Healthcare, And A Tribute To Uwe Reinhardt.*" Health Affairs 38, no. 1 (2019): 87–95.

diabetes (which accounts for one in four dollars spent on healthcare), cancer, and heart disease.

In summary, the US does not use its very, very large healthcare budget effectively. The goal with every dollar spent on healthcare is to receive positive health outcomes resulting in a return on investment (ROI). That ROI value is derived from a healthy, happy population—and, compared to other countries, we are failing in this area.

Patient experience and interaction with the system is essential to the cost and quality issue, and is probably more relevant to most readers. What drives that experience? Incentives and clinical practice model paradigms. Incentives are built into the system from a high level, and the ways in which the patient-facing part of the system forms itself around those incentives impact what the patient experiences. These incentives come in several forms, but are primarily based in finance and the ways in which we pay for health services.

Clinical practice model paradigms are the ways in which the knowledge of medicine is provided to patients. This has been done in largely the same way for hundreds of years. Patient gets sick, patient calls doctor, patient gets treatment, patient is sent home until something else happens.

One of the key points that gets lost when discussing large reform efforts is that in order to improve health outcomes, something about the patient-system interaction must change. There needs to be a discernable patient-based end result out of whatever innovations, policies, or changes are made.

The assumption is often made that the way in which patients receive healthcare services from the system is fine—it is simply a matter of ensuring coverage, access, and assigning the proper treatments. But this assumption has not produced results for people who are already covered.

Fortunately, the methods by which we pay for healthcare and the places in which we invest our national healthcare dollar can be changed and altered to enhance the entire system's performance, and, most importantly, the experience of the patient within it—or, rather, the "user" of the system to borrow from the user-experience design-thinking field.

\* \* \*

Healthcare reform is tough because of the size of the industry, the ways in which we approach major change currently, and the deep level of institutional inertia that exists within it.

"People hold onto the image they have of healthcare so tightly—especially clinicians and physicians. Reform is inherently a paradigm shift," Dan Skinner said with unparalleled passion and enthusiasm over the phone.

I met Dan on Twitter. I was attending the Academy Health Annual Research Meeting (or, the ARM for short) this past June where Dan and I interacted regularly on Twitter (as is becoming more commonplace during conferences). Academy Health is one of the preeminent organizations that promotes health services research, or the field that studies the health system. It is a combination of medicine, economics, management, finance, policy, and political science with a healthcare twist. While I have never met Dan in person, he and I share similar views on healthcare reform that became very evident after I set up a call with him through a Twitter direct message.

Dan is a recently tenured professor at Ohio University, where he teaches medical students and studies the healthcare system. He is a political scientist by training. Fortunately for me, "recently tenured" means that he is willing to speak freely about the healthcare system and its inherent problems in a truly authentic way.

Dan works with his students on many things, but often focuses on distinguishing between *aversion to change* and *real legitimate clinical critiques from older physicians.* Just like most industries, the new workforce is trained by the old workforce. This is a problem in healthcare because the institutionalization and aversion to change are incredibly strong in a way that inhibits changes to existing models.

"The medical education system does not promote innovation, it promotes tradition," says Dan.

One cannot affect patient-level change if the people providing the services are so deeply tied to the way things have always been done. Herein lies one of the core issues facing healthcare innovators and reformers.

Dan elaborates on this: "In many cases, I have noticed that medical students and physicians are the same things that their identity is staked within. It is a paradox. The long hours, the pressure, the heroic identity are all threatened by change and transformation. There is a tension between physician identity and what physicians hate about the system itself. They hold onto the bad parts of medicine, the bad rites of passage, and are frustrated with the system at the same time. Medicine is an institution and it says to new members, 'who are you to have it better than me.'"

Rather than change the system for good, the medical institution is both resistant to change and frustrated by lack of change at the same time, due to this institutional inertia and core identity problem. Physicians love to suffer, make their future members suffer as they did, and fight hard to maintain the suffering because it is a part of the culture and it's "how we do Medicine and healthcare."

"This really affects the system's ability to change," says Dan with a bit of a chuckle.

Now, there are plenty of innovative physicians out there and leaders, like Dan, who are trying to change this culture. Physicians are the best example but other fields under the healthcare umbrella also experience the "well, we have always done it this way" effect. Inertia in institutions and "cults of healthcare" culture are thus barriers to innovation.

"I tell them that maybe it's that you don't get sued enough, or maybe that you get paid too much. When the older docs talk about the good ole days, the truth is that they did not have very good outcomes. We are doing system innovation, it is happening, and we need to talk honestly about what the older physicians were able to achieve," Dan explains, discussing changes to the way healthcare is delivered and the role of the physician.

Physicians often express frustration with change and burn-out is a huge issue because of tension between the old ways and new innovations. These innovations are happening *around the physicians* such as health services researchers, healthcare managers, and healthcare consultants. Whether changes by these groups produces benefits is questionable, but innovation is occurring *around* physicians instead of *with* them. And, just like physicians, many institutions and professional fields in healthcare struggle to adopt new technologies, innovations, and models because of strong inertia.

Dan's passion for this subject, like many of us passionate about healthcare innovation, comes out of personal experience. During the ACA debate in 2009, Dan was diagnosed with a form of cancer and "the debate became framed in this very personal stake." He is one of many academic researchers who study healthcare and teach the next generation of leaders to take a different view of healthcare by changing their philosophies and mental images of the way healthcare works.

The system is managed and maintained by a huge array of both competing and aligned interests, politics, and profit motives. But collectively, they all measure, maintain, and attempt to affect the same variables. At a basic level, those variables can be reduced to "cost" and "quality." Cost is how much is spent on services by patients, organizations, employers, and the government; and quality is how well patients fare in the system in both their experiences and actual health outcomes.

These are the two major shortcomings of the US healthcare system as a whole.

While variables, economics, and academic research are exciting to some of us, this book will focus specifically on innovations that can reach and impact the patient experience. Through this research, we know many of the problems, pain points, and issues.

What we need is a mindset shift for politicians, individuals, policymakers, healthcare executives, and everyone involved in the system. We need something that one might call "a major philosophy shift" and to refocus largescale reform efforts on impactful innovations that can truly affect the ways in which patient meets healthcare services.

\* \* \*

The healthcare system is one giant workaround. The actual design of the system does not solve for the objective: producing a healthier population. The system needs a reorientation or a flip. This is not going to occur from any sweeping legislation or reform, but rather from thousands of well-designed innovations that alter the ways in which the system cares for patients with chronic illness.

Large-scale system reform is exciting and, therefore, it is so easy to jump to national and sweeping reform. I have talked about my interest in large-scale healthcare system reform and transformation for years, but the fact is that it is simply too challenging to tackle all at once due to the unparalleled complexity and segmentation of the healthcare system. The changes that typically happen at the large-scale often fail to filter down to patient-level where improvement must occur— not to mention the political issue of administration change affecting previous administrations' progress.

Smaller, more focused, and less politically driven change is thus likely to be more effective at changing patients' experiences and outcomes.

For years, election campaigns bring up discussions around Medicare-for-All. This is a movement hoping to solve all of our nation's healthcare problems through sweeping national legislation. This is a big effort (and one that is discussed on television by politicians who have little concept of how healthcare actually works). Without diving into all the details of what this would look like, I would argue that this move would have little effect on many of the current problems plaguing the system right now.

Unless the bill contains major changes to how the system and patients interact, the bill is making changes at levels too high and far-removed from actual patients. Apart from providing universal healthcare coverage—which is by no means a bad thing—this move does not necessarily mean much would change about the patient-level experience. If the goal of healthcare system reform is a healthier population within reasonable cost, then, logically, change must occur that affects the ways in which patients receive their care.

Our most recent national attempt at healthcare reform came under the ACA. Some of the changes made under the ACA reduced cost in some estimations and in some areas may have improved certain health outcomes, but the ways in which the patient receives health services from the system did not change significantly.

The patient still goes to the system when something goes wrong, or maybe, once a year for a wellness visit—this time, though, thanks to the ACA, they may have a bit more coverage for preventive services. Some people who were unable to get health coverage now are able to access care because of Medicaid coverage expansions and the development of the individual market for health insurance.[6]

Health coverage is good, but for those who already have it the system still does not deliver care services to patients in an effective manner. More people with coverage actually adds more cost to the nation because more people will utilize care under said coverage.

Without changes at the patient-system level, we will keep spending more and getting less because the underlying problem has not been solved. Will there be benefits seen from universal coverage? Yes. We know that health insurance access does result in improved health. But this impact has its limits and will eventually stop producing benefits after reaching a certain point, unless there are changes to the delivery system to better care for patients with chronic illness.

In the US, about 90 percent of the population has health insurance coverage.[7] The immediate effect of Medicare-for-All legislation would be to bring the coverage rate closer to the 100 percent level. This is a great thing. But this alone would do little to impact the frontlines of the patient-system healthcare experience, aside from getting some currently

---

6   See the exchanges at healthcare.gov
7   Berchick, Edward R., Emily Hood, and Jessica C. Barnett, Current Population Reports, P60-264, Health Insurance Coverage in the United States: 2017, US Government Printing Office, Washington, DC, 2018

un-covered individuals healthcare coverage and therefore access to preventive services and screenings like flu shots and cholesterol tests.

Again, this is good. But unless the actual delivery of care to those individuals changes to better manage patient medical conditions that are discovered during these new preventive services, this effect will show marginal improvement and will reach a "peak benefit" as those individuals without coverage, who gain it, will see some improvements in their health. This was observed in some populations after the ACA was implemented.

Universal coverage, while good and a precursor to patients interacting with the health system, is not the silver bullet that will solve healthcare problems.

The opposition to this point of view would argue that a major reform bill of this magnitude would contain a significant amount of additional alterations to the system. These add-ons to the legislation would be areas where small things could be identified and addressed—much like how Unite Us built a tool to connect CBOs, such as payment method changes, or changing the models and methods by which patient meets system, or patient meets physician (or other providers). The allocation of funding through our nation's federal research and development programs would also be a benefit of this type of major legislation, but again, the actual innovation occurs at a much smaller level with support from this funding.

When we try to tackle the full health system, we lose sight of the patient-system interaction. Changes need to operate at a micro-level to actually influence the ways in which care is provided to patients. This is the end goal and the point at which health improvements can be made. Small, focused, and well-designed improvements and innovations are able to affect this interaction to alter the ways in which patients are guided toward wellness.

Chronic disease is the problem and the existing models of healthcare services to manage these conditions are inadequate, thus resulting in high spending due to preventable episodes of care. Innovations that can fundamentally change some aspects of how these services are rendered to patients with chronic illness are ones that have the ability to reduce the demand for health services and to improve the health and wellbeing of the population. Coverage is helpful, but largescale reform will require going beyond this point to reach the patient with new innovations.

# CHAPTER 2

# A BRIEF HISTORY

———

To better understand how innovations can fuel disruption and scalable change in healthcare, it is important to briefly discuss the formative context in which our current healthcare system grew up—so as to understand what the primary major issue is when it comes to delivery system changes.

Our healthcare system today is a product of its historical formation from a time where there was comparatively very little medical knowledge or technology to be applied to humanity's ailments. A lot of people died. It was not a healthy time. When thinking about the historical formation of our current healthcare system, you can think of the last hundred years or so as a "pioneer-esque" covered wagon, traveling down the dirt road of time.

This wagon gets people from point A to point B, albeit slowly, but it gets the job done. As the wagon keeps moving along the dirt road of time, it both starts to fall apart and requires patchwork and on-the-go repairs to keep moving along toward point B. This process occurs during the whole length of the journey, with new add-ons to try to improve the wagon.

While this wagon is still being used, new technologies have been developed. Here I'm speaking of industrialization: the internal combustion engine, paved roads, cars, the Tesla Model S, solar power, and plastics. These things have been added to the wagon and the wagon has adapted to these new technologies, but the fact is that it is still a covered wagon on a dirt road. Maybe it has solar panels on its roof and is riding along next to a Tesla, but again, it is still a covered wagon.

Our "covered-wagon" healthcare system is still operating under the same models as long ago, despite its failure to modify alongside new technologies.

* * *

There are two areas that are important to highlight when thinking about key historical elements in the formation of the healthcare system we know today.

First, the capabilities of medicine itself. It is important to distinguish the distinct role of the institution/discipline of medicine (the stuff doctors learn in medical school) and the health system itself; while they are interdependent, they have unique and individual evolutions that are important to acknowledge.

This book is about the health payment and delivery system; i.e. connecting the patient with medical expertise and treatments. The system allows medical knowledge to reach the patient to attempt to improve their health. The system is the way in which healthcare is paid for, and the methods and places by which it provides services to patients. We, in the business, typically separate the health system into the payment side (health insurance, Medicare, Medicaid) and the delivery side (physicians, hospitals, clinics, and other, typically, institution-based organizations).

When looking back to the origins of the health **system**, it is important to begin with health insurance. At the beginning existed accident policies and other structures that loosely resemble the health insurance-type institutions that we know today.

In the late 1800s, employers began to offer disability policies for industrial workers injured on the job (working in the early industrial US was dangerous), and, who could therefore, could no longer work, or accident policies that would provide some basic financial protection if an injury occurred. In the decades following the Industrial Revolution, where accidents were common and big machines could swallow limbs, this made a lot of sense.

During this time, accidents and major illnesses were cared for in hospitals when people were close to death's door. Our system was built to deal with these types of episodes, accidents, and severe illnesses rather than the common chronic illnesses that drive today's spending.

The first accident policy was offered by the Franklin Health Assurance Company of Massachusetts, founded in 1850. This seems like a pretty common benefit today, but back then, this was a novel method by which employers were able to differentiate themselves to attract employees. Thankfully, the field of occupational health and safety has driven a lot of improvement when it comes to accidents in the workplace. These types of insurance were designed for "catastrophic" issues that may occur for an individual. But at the time, there was a problem.

Medicine was the problem. In the early 1900s, not a lot of value could be added by medicine when compared to our medical capabilities today. Doctors made house calls, and were still largely independent and community-based. There were no MRI machines, very few sophisticated lab tests, no surgical robots, and even fewer treatments for many diseases. At the same time, these community-based doctors were paid for out-of-pocket by their patients at reasonable rates. These are the community doctors you think of from long ago with black bags and tweed suits, showing up to make a house call.

Doctors were individuals within their communities; occasionally groups of doctors would get together to convince a community to build a hospital for them to care for their sickest patients and those injured. Since before the Middle Ages, hospitals were places that the sickest or most injured patients went to die. Sorry for the morbid outlook, but at the time, that was the truth. Medicine, from the mid-1850s to the early 1900s, was simply not able to do many of the things we can do today. The biggest cause of death during the American Civil War wasn't direct physical violence— it was infection from wounds.

During the evolution of the **system**, hospitals began offering a pre-paid number of hospital beds to employer organizations to offer as a benefit to their employees. One of the first examples of this is a teacher-formed hospitalization plan in Dallas, Texas formed in 1929.[8]

Again, at this point, most expenses were covered by individual patients unless they needed to be hospitalized for a period of time for which their pre-paid hospitalization plan would cover their stay. There was really no need for anything else because medicine itself was not at the point where it could provide a wide range of services.

Today, we are accomplishing incredible medical feats. For example, on December 4th, 2018 Dr. Dani Ejsenberg led a team that produced the first baby born to a woman who received a uterus transplant from a deceased donor (much like how we perform organ transplants for kidneys and livers). Think about that. Someone who was previously unable to have a baby due to a problem with or absence of a uterus was able to have a baby from a transplanted uterus from another person.

Or when Gilead Sciences received approval for the drug, Harvoni, to be used to cure hepatitis C. Yeah, that's right, *cure*. Medical science has provided the ability to cure hepatitis C, a disease that has been around causing suffering for hundreds of years. Pharmaceutical and biotechnology innovation merits its own book, and I will not focus on issues like drug prices in this book.

8    Buchmueller, Thomas C.; Monheit, Alan C. (2009). "Employer-Sponsored Health Insurance and the Promise of Health Insurance Reform". *Inquiry.* **46** (2): 187–202.

Back in the early 1900s, we did not even have antibiotics. It wasn't until 1928 that Alexander Fleming made the somewhat-accidental discovery that a mold secretion growing in a petri dish killed Staphylococcus bacteria. Thus, penicillin—the cure for your strep throat and sinus infections—was born. Before 1928, people were showing up to hospitals to die of pneumonia and infections derived from an accidental cut from a knife in the kitchen. Truly, medicine could not do much.

Now, we can do a lot of things. We are not invincible, but we have a lot of medical knowledge and treatments available. Diabetics can control their blood sugar with insulin injections. Individuals with cancer now have some options to treat, and sometimes cure, their disease. Children with asthma can manage their disease with an inhaler. Congestive heart failure patients can take medications to control the fluid impacting their heart. People with high blood pressure can take drugs that lower it to healthy and livable levels.

In recent years, medical technology has advanced to incredible places that now offer the opportunity to truly improve the health of so many people. The challenge, now, is how can we both pay for and connect the patient with the treatments they need most effectively and efficiently.

With medicine reaching this point, the healthcare system—the ways by which we pay for and deliver medicine to the patients—needs to think about its problems differently. We are still largely operating under the same system orientation that began in the early 1900s. We are still a covered wagon, with some flashy new technologies, but a covered wagon nonetheless. Patients get sick, come to the doctor or hospital, receive treatment, and then gets sent on their way to follow discharge instructions.

Over the past century, these "catastrophic insurance policies" turned into the more comprehensive coverage we have today. In the mid-20th century, Medicare and Medicaid programs were passed into law and a new paradigm was established: the idea of healthcare coverage as a possibility and even an entitlement. Health insurance began to cover expenses and to take financial risk for the health utilization of members. No longer was the purpose of this insurance to be a protection against catastrophic and financially significant health events. Now, the insurance pays for more common things like medications, physician visits, hospital stays, medical imaging, laboratory tests, and so much more.

This is probably good for society. The nation reaps value when its citizens are healthy and able to work and produce a benefit to the GDP and quality of life. Remember, despite the rat race, inequality, and struggles of life, the ultimate goal here is to allow people to live happy, healthy, free lives. This tends not to include spending quality time in waiting rooms, hospital beds, and exam tables.

Due to research and government investment, insurance companies and other government payment programs learned quickly that they can make more money, or save more money, if they cover certain things that clearly kept people healthy and reduced risk factors for bad outcomes, disease, and therefore higher spending out of the pool of insurance money. One of the common examples of this type of service is an annual check-up with a primary care physician.

For many people, particularly young people, this is one of the only points of interaction with the health system. Thus, this is an opportunity for insurance companies to get ahead to make sure that this patient is healthy and that there are no glaring health issues or behaviors that need to be addressed. If something is identified, such as high cholesterol, then a plan can be worked out to handle this before the person ends up with a clogged artery after years of undiagnosed high cholesterol and costs $1million after a major ischemic stroke event. In the long-term, and, over many patients, this can help protect the insurance company from having to pay for someone getting really sick when it could have been prevented by earlier intervention. This is an attempt at being more of a proactive system, but it still doesn't go far enough.

So, here we are today with insurance companies that cover *some* important preventive services that they hope will keep their entire patient population a little healthier, resulting in savings, and, therefore, profit/savings for them. But now we know that medicine itself has advanced to a point where there is a treatment or service for thousands of conditions. There now exists a tension between insurance coverage and treatments that provide a benefit to patients.

Included in this new tension and coverage of many healthcare expenses is the way in which the actual providers of the services are paid. Remember my earlier mention of incentives?

That brings me to a brief introduction of the payment side of healthcare. That is, how physicians and hospitals are paid for providing services to you.

* * *

There is a loose differentiation between the payment side of healthcare and the delivery side. Delivery is the patient care services-producing side, and it may surprise you that hospitals and physicians like to actually be paid for the care they *deliver*.

Well, the way in which payment for most healthcare services in the country is performed is through a system called Fee-for-Service (FFS). Essentially, when you go to your annual check-up with your primary care physician, that physician submits a numbered code to your insurance company (or Medicare/Medicaid) for the service performed. Then they get paid a pre-determined rate for that code, and money flows from insurer to the service provider.

If you are a physician or a hospital CEO, what do you think you want to do under this system? Well, if you are interested in making money, like most people, your job is to get as many patients into your facility as possible for a check-up, procedure, overnight stay, and other services. Getting truly cynical, your company makes more money if people are sicker because they need your services more.

Now, I am not saying that your doctor wants you to be sick or that hospital managers want their community to be worse off. I am, however, saying that if a doctor wants to keep their doors open and lights on, then patient demand is required.

This incentive in the system is one of the root causes of the cost issue today. And anything that has to do with money becomes a giant political issue, and thus large-scale change becomes difficult.

When it comes to keeping the country healthy, insurance coverage for important and effective services is crucial but expensive—especially when the organizations performing the services want to drive a high volume. The heart of today's health cost crisis is rooted in the system's evolution. At a conceptual level, the country wants to keep its people healthy. Employers want healthy workers to drive productivity because the national economy benefits from healthy, happy, productive workers, and, quite honestly, a society is measured by how well it takes care of its citizens.

Our basic goal, as a country, is to pay for wellness and health for as many people as possible for the lowest amount of money—that's getting more value for each dollar spent. To do this, though, the healthcare system needs to provide the right patient with the right services.

Under our traditional and current payment incentives, there are many unnecessary services provided for a number of reasons, But, at a certain level, it comes down to the method by which we pay for healthcare services—FFS.

In combination with the FFS conundrum, our system is still operating under the principles by which it was formed. The "catastrophic-based" system is still the foundation by which we provide healthcare services. Only when people start to feel poorly, get injured, or show up to their once-a-year, fifteen-minute primary care visit does the system step in to provide needed services for that patient—often, though, this manifests as too many services because under FFS, it's possible to make more money.

**This is an episodic, catastrophic, and reactive-oriented system that incentivizes lots of services to be provided, generating wasteful services that do not add much value to actual health.**

This is a problem, especially as we now have the ability to manage many chronic conditions that used to kill people. Now, health services are required to maintain health more frequently than accidental or near-death episodes. Medicine has made it possible to treat these conditions, but the system has not developed models to adequately assist patients in managing them in daily life.

In addition to not adequately supporting patients with chronic illness, FFS payment coupled with existing delivery models generates waste. Much of the ability of the healthcare system to reduce costs under FFS comes from reducing unnecessary and wasteful care provided to patients. You may not need that second MRI or that specialist referral because it will not help you attain better health—there is thus no value in those services. This gets into a larger discussion about fraud, waste, abuse, malpractice, defensive medicine, and other incentives built into the system outside of finance. This book, though, is about positively impacting patient health to reduce costs, so I will not discuss those topics directly.

One of the key reasons why people hate insurance companies is that they deny payment for care or try to keep you from going to the emergency room. These types of activities, while they seem malicious (and often can be) are, in theory, designed to steer people to more cost-effective and appropriate locations to receive healthcare services. It is much cheaper to send someone to a primary care doctor (~$100) than an emergency department (~$1000).

This approach is a quick and easy way to reduce care costs and is not necessarily a bad thing. Due to strict policies in companies, horror stories about care denial do occur and there are terrible situations for everyone involved in these situations. Steerage to more appropriate levels of care is likely a good thing, but rationing or payment denial for services that are necessary is, obviously, a bad thing.

What needs to happen is a shift in mindset, incentives, and the adoption of technologies that enable payment and delivery systems to actually save money from improving patient care, so they do not demand medical services and do not need to be denied coverage in order to prevent services from being rendered.

If the system works to help keep people healthy, then denial and steerage are not the drivers of cost savings, but rather the actual demand for healthcare services is reduced. This is the holy grail for healthcare, and many people think this is not possible. Right now, we do not have validated, cost-effective, and highly scalable methods by which we can reliably improve outcomes for all patients. But that is beginning to change as technology is developed to better deliver care across numerous facets.

What if we could flip the system to generate the outcomes we want to see in a manner that is proactive and supportive for patients with chronic illness, rather than one that is reactive?

Far too often, we see the health system as something we hope we never need. But what if the system was able to help keep you from needing it? What if our healthcare system worked proactively instead of reactively? What if your doctor was paid to keep you healthy instead of when you showing up due to extant sickness? What if your hospital did not want to fill its beds with patients, but instead wanted to keep people in their homes and in their communities? What if the system was able to provide effective and passive services before you end up admitted to the hospital because something got out of control? **That is what this book is about—innovations that drive fundamental disruption toward a system like this.**

So, how can this happen?

It *is* possible for this to occur, and, in many cases, it already is slowly occurring across the country. This is not a futuristic vision. We have the technology and avenues through which this can be accomplished. In fact, there are many people who have been working their whole lives to accomplish reform along these lines. The most successful people working to do these things share some common characteristics. They often have a lived experience that drives passion to solve some deeply rooted problems, they have taken a systems approach looking outside their organization's current scope, they use design thinking to build, and, most importantly, they do not try to bite off too much at one time—they try to solve manageable and important problems that drive change at the patient-level.

Over the last chapter, I have greatly simplified the history and moving parts of the healthcare system. There are many nuances, complications, and significant variations across the nation in how the system operates. But, by and large, the issues I have raised are key to understanding how our healthcare system is being transformed and the type of disruption that is occurring in one of the most important industries in human history.

What is more important than the collective happiness, healthy families, and humans helping other humans in healthcare?

The innovators and future healthcare leaders making a big splash into healthcare's slow-to-innovate culture and poor track record are thinking outside-the-box about the little things that can make a big difference for the patient. Far too often we discuss Medicare-for-All scope ideas. We pass bills like the ACA to "fix healthcare." But, again, at a patient-level, very little has changed in the ways we connect medicine to the patient.

We still have a yearly physical, show up to the emergency department after getting sicker, and have very little support when it comes to managing health conditions in our daily lives. We still have to see separate physicians who have separate records, get asked the same questions all the time, and are left on our own to navigate our own health.

Big, sweeping reform is exciting and we like to think that these things can make a huge difference in our individual experience, but some of the most successful disruptors in the world have been small things that produce a big impact and that are so well-designed for the end-user that institutional inertia cannot stop them.

Small things connect together with many other small things to harness collective power. Small things can be designed so well that they fundamentally alter the ways in which systems operate. And, for our purposes, most importantly, small things can affect change at the patient-level.

Sweeping reform is cool, flashy, inspiring, and makes for a great re-election campaign, but I will tell you that a Medicare-for-All-type solution will impact the average person very much the same way that the ACA did. The ACA was reasonably successful at increasing health insurance coverage (or would have been if all individual states had jumped on board). Truthfully, most people, aside from the few percentage points that gained healthcare coverage, did not feel a significant change to the way they experienced healthcare services. In fact, our failure to change the way we deliver care in this country has actually made things worse as premiums continue to climb and our expenditures continue to grow out of control.

To affect change at the patient-level, the type of innovation that actually has the ability to improve health, it is necessary to think differently about the healthcare system. It is necessary to think across independent disciplines and organizations to identify the small changes that can be made to truly knock the ball out of the park.

The healthcare system is a complicated and massive institution. These small things are thus not inexpensive or easy to do. Rather, they are small in that they do not try to do everything at once. This enables strong, precise innovation so well-designed that large institutions cannot compete with existing models because the new ones are so much more effective.

Just like Taylor and Unite Us did not build a large multi-faceted organization to solve everyone's social problems and figure out a way to pay for them, necessary healthcare system innovations need not be comprehensive solutions. They just need to be the enablers of a larger impact.

To not just improve the covered wagon, but to toss it off the dirt road and introduce a Tesla Model S, will require a change in the way we think about healthcare delivery, our payment models and their incentives, and the use of new digital health technologies that have seen slow adoption in the system.

## CHAPTER 3

# THE DEMAND PROBLEM

---

I remember walking into sixth grade one August morning in Marietta, Georgia thinking, *What am I doing here?* as I specifically chose to wear my backpack over just my right shoulder (because that's what I thought I should do now that I was in middle school). I had to be different and cool. I also remember meeting a lot of new people for the first time, as my elementary school merged with another one when reaching sixth grade. This is where I first met Morgan and her twin sister Meagan. Since then, Morgan has attended the University of Georgia where she is finishing up a degree in accounting. But Morgan has also experienced a great deal more than most college students her age when it comes to the health system.

When Morgan was seven years old, she ended up in a local hospital in Marietta (the same one in which I was born) where, after a three-day stay, she was diagnosed with Type-1 diabetes and her world would change forever. She and her family found out that she was going to live with this disease and its necessary daily maintenance for the rest of her life.

Type-1 diabetes is a lifelong condition where a person's pancreas is unable to produce insulin needed to regulate and maintain the body's blood sugar level—it falls under the broad category called a "chronic condition." If blood sugar gets out of the proper range, whether high or low, it causes tremendous issues in the body, is life-threatening, and often requires hospitalizations or emergency department visits.

During Morgan and her family's initial three-day stay in the hospital, they were introduced to a disease that would be present for Morgan's lifetime. She and her family were taught important skills in the management of the disease to allow her to live her life outside of the healthcare system.

"They gave me a teddy bear to practice pricking my finger and giving shots, while my parents were taught how to manage the condition by physicians and diabetes educators," Morgan recalled as she told her story.

There are two types of diabetes, Type 1 and Type 2. Morgan is in the category of Type 1 of which the cause is not yet concretely known. Type 2 is related to lifestyle and obesity and combined—both types are responsible for the one out of four dollars spent on healthcare in the United States. Like many other lifelong conditions, diabetes can be managed. While a hassle for patients, daily self-management is possible with the assistance of insulin and other medications, lifestyle changes, dietary changes, and constant vigilance.

It may be counterintuitive, but the car crashes, dramatic injuries, and scary incidents that we hear so much about on the news and social media are actually not driving the majority of spending in the US health system. As I've previously mentioned, the cost and quality problems lie with chronic conditions and their management and prevention.

While car crash patients often have extremely expensive episodes of care due to emergency department visits, surgical procedures, life-supporting measures, and other intensive treatments, they do not occur frequently enough to drive the majority of our healthcare spending. In fact, our health system is oriented quite well to deal with these types of issues. Both our payment and delivery systems are designed to deal with this type of low-frequency, catastrophic medical event. If rare accidents, snake bites, and shark attacks were the most common conditions seen by our health system, it would work very well.

A rare, one-time, and intensive episode of care in an individual's life is exactly what early health insurance was designed to handle and our episodic, institution-based health system was designed to manage.

Unfortunately, diseases like hypertension (high blood pressure), high cholesterol, heart disease, asthma, cancers, dementia, and diabetes are to blame for our out of control health expenditures. They are extremely prevalent in the US.[9] According to 2015 data, approximately half of US adults suffered from a chronic condition and 25 percent had multiple

---

9    Sambamoorthi, Usha, Xi Tan, and Arijita Deb. 2015. "Multiple Chronic Conditions and Healthcare Costs among Adults." *Expert Review of Pharmacoeconomics and Outcomes Research* 15 (5): 823–32.

co-occurring chronic conditions (MCC).[10] That's pretty substantial. Half of US adults have some form of chronic illness that requires management over a lifetime.

It's no wonder that chronic conditions are associated with 75 percent of overall healthcare spending. The spending is allocated to daily treatments and medications needed to manage the condition and more frequent outpatient visits over a lifetime. But the real costs come from a failure to manage the conditions and the resulting emergency department and inpatient care that comes when conditions are not properly managed.

The problem lies not in the capabilities of medicine to treat these conditions. Biomedical research has produced medications, treatments, and behavior changes that can be effective for many of them.

The problem instead lies in the ways in which the healthcare payment system incentivizes care for patients and orientation of the institution-based delivery system that affects how a patient receives medical knowledge and treatments.

\* \* \*

If you take a deeper look at the patients who cost the most, have the worst outcomes, and present the best opportunity for which to improve care, you find the "high-cost, super-utilizers."

---

10   Castaño, Adam, and Mathew S Maurer. 2015. "Multiple Chronic Conditions and Labor Force Outcomes: A Population Study of US Adults." *American Journal of Medicine* 20 (2): 163–78.

High-risk patients with multiple chronic conditions drive the majority of cost, due to their utilization of costly points of care such as emergency services and inpatient hospitalizations.

In a study looking at "high-cost super-utilizers," 59 percent of them had at least two chronic conditions.[11] During the course of the study, patients experienced an average of 3.2 inpatient hospital stays and 2.8 emergency room visits during the one-year study period.

Imagine going to the ER and being admitted to the hospital that many times in one year. Twenty-six percent of patients experienced one or more readmissions within thirty days of being discharged from the hospital. This "thirty-day readmissions metric" was introduced after the ACA to incentivize hospitals to provide better care and to prevent readmissions to a facility that was supposed to ensure the patient was better.

This metric makes sense, but is very complicated when dealing with high-risk patients. Hospitals often argue that they do not have control of the patient's behavior once they are discharged from the hospital and therefore should not be responsible for poor adherence to discharge instructions (recommendations made by the treating physician for the patient once they leave the facility). My former colleague and experienced nurse, Amy Mueller, once told me that "a patient who just had heart surgery can go home

11    Harris, L. Jeff, Ilana Graetz, Pradeep S.B. Podila, Jim Wan, Teresa M. Waters, and James E. Bailey. 2016. "Characteristics of Hospital and Emergency Care Super-Utilizers with Multiple Chronic Conditions." *Journal of Emergency Medicine* 50 (4): e203–14.

and start smoking again and there is nothing that the system can do to stop them."

At the same time, it is important that when a patient is admitted to a hospital, they receive care that adds value to their health, and, upon release, should be in better condition than when first admitted. As one simple example of how the system can become more proactive, for patients like those described by Amy, hospitals have tried to identify smokers and get them into cessation programs prior to discharge. But again, according to the study looking at these super-utilizers, 26 percent of them left the hospital and were right back in within a month.

The reliance on the same models by the delivery system keeps these patients coming back to the hospital after discharge because hospitals really have no reason to do anything extra to prevent it if they get paid again. Under traditional FFS, this is the reality. Under the ACA, thirty-day readmission rates began to be measured and tied to payments, to attempt to incentivize hospitals toward actions like the smoking cessation program intervention. These types of incentives have the power to change the behavior and models by which delivery organizations provide care to patients.

These findings from the study elucidate the major underlying services that drive costs derived from patients with chronic illness. While the study cannot be generalized to the entire country, this evidence shows the ways in which patients with chronic conditions utilize costly service lines to produce higher national healthcare costs.

This is the primary driver of demand for health services. Healthy people do not require high-intensity, high-cost services. Healthy people require relatively low-cost preventive and maintenance services. Rather than simply fixing prices or rationing care, it is possible to solve for the underlying root cause of costly health service utilization.

As patients with complex diseases or multiple chronic conditions deteriorate due to poor disease management, they seek help at emergency rooms, additional physician appointments, and may even require admission to the hospital to receive high-cost treatments and procedures. All of these things contribute heavily to the cost of the system—*preventable cost* to the system, in many cases.

\* \* \*

Chronic conditions develop from a wide variety of risk factors and individual behaviors—the choices we make and lifestyles we live affect our health. Everyone knows that eating vegetables and exercise are healthy things to do. We call those positive health behaviors. But there are also negative health behaviors or risk factors. These are things like living a sedentary lifestyle and eating a poor diet—in other words, sitting on the couch watching *The Office* for the twelfth time while indulging in that Trader Joe's Mac 'n Cheese (I'm guilty) is a risk factor for the development of chronic diseases like Type 2 diabetes, heart disease, and other conditions.

Common risk factors can be behavioral, or physiological, such as obesity, smoking, living a sedentary lifestyle, eating a diet lacking fruits and vegetables, having high cholesterol, or a combination of factors.[12]

We know this. Everyone remembers the food pyramid from elementary school. We know we shouldn't eat ice cream for breakfast or have French fries with every meal. But too often, we do it anyway. Individual health behaviors drive a lot of the formation and development of chronic disease. These choices, particularly those of diet and exercise, can be individual decisions and habits or as a result of a lack of education, poverty, or availability of healthy choices in an area.

Risk factors for chronic diseases can also be genetic, though, as a field, medicine and public health sciences have moved away from a strictly genetic lens. When it comes down to it, a person's health is affected by so many things, behaviors, the environment, social factors, human interaction, and the entire experience of life.

Genetic components may act as a risk factor for certain conditions, but just as genetics can be a risk factor, it can also be influenced by these other factors. Environmental, social, lifestyle, and other experiences can influence the expression of genes toward a condition, as well.

That brings me back to Morgan. Now I am by no means a physician or an expert, but her Type 1 diabetes, while a chronic condition, did not come from her behaviors. It is unclear where it came from, though it may be rooted in genetics.

---

12    Adams, Mary L., Joseph Grandpre, David L. Katz, and Douglas Shenson. 2019. "The Impact of Key Modifiable Risk Factors on Leading Chronic Conditions." *Preventive Medicine* 120 (June 2018)

\* \* \*

One of the most recent health system fads is a concept called "the social determinants of health." I call this a fad not because it lacks importance—it is tremendously important—but because I hope to leave you with the idea that these concepts are self-evident. The research that has been performed in this area is important to gain widespread adoption, to understand the issue, and to develop programs, but the core concept hardly needs research to understand.

Just like individual health behaviors and lifestyle risk factors, like that bag of Doritos I just finished, risk factors can also be psycho-socio-economic such as low income, low educational attainment, lack of access to healthcare, housing insecurity, food insecurity, experience with interpersonal violence, previous incarceration, presence of discrimination, and other social factors.[13]

These factors are becoming increasingly popular topics of discussion in health policy and health system reform because they are major drivers of the development and exacerbation of chronic conditions, and, therefore, of cost and quality.

The World Health Organization (WHO) defines the social determinants of health as "the conditions in which people are born, grow, work, live, and age and the set of forces and systems shaping the conditions of daily life."[14] As innovation and reform of the system take place, it is necessary to address

13   Ibid.
14   Cockerham, William C., Bryant W. Hamby, and Gabriela R. Oates. 2017. "The Social Determinants of Chronic Disease." *American Journal of Preventive Medicine* 52 (1): S5–12.

the prevention of these psycho-socio-economic factors that contribute to the formation and exacerbation of chronic illness leading to increased health expenditures.

These "social determinants of health" contribute to the formation and exacerbation of chronic illness in the population and present both an opportunity to innovate due to the significant impact on cost associated with these factors.

The highest-cost patients in the country are burdened by high psycho-socio-economic risk factors impacting their ability to self-manage and navigate the health system, as well as providing causal factors for their illness in the first place. They have existing chronic illnesses, are poor, and often older.

Most chronic illness occurs in older people. We know that the Medicare population (US citizens age 65+) has rates of chronic illness in greater than 66 percent of people. This makes sense as there are not many eighteen-year-olds walking around with chronic obstructive pulmonary disorder (COPD), general heart disease, or congestive heart failure, save a rare genetic-linked condition or accident.

In addition to and in combination with, chronic illness occurs frequently in the Medicaid population (the poorest people in the country), or individuals with low incomes, living in poor neighborhoods, without equitable access or means to adequately manage their health. This is primarily due to the presence of risk factors like the above outlined social determinants of health.

I do not like the commoditization of these social factors, but if it encourages a wider view of health and a transition to addressing the problems, I say the ends justify the means. To me, the "social determinants of health" are a digestible way to reduce the experience of poverty. This isn't a new concept. Poor people are not able to be healthy—this is a story as old as time.

In our mission to alter the delivery of healthcare toward helping patients manage their chronic conditions and prevent their formation altogether in a more proactive way, the way in which the patient meets the system must change.

We want to keep people healthy. A person cannot be healthy if they are struggling to pay rent, taking care of three children as a single parent, using money that they don't have to try and feed their family, and then also attempting to manage health. Building a better healthcare delivery system requires an understanding of patient-user problems such as this. And, for the cost and quality crisis, it is important to look at the high-cost super-utilizers and to build a system that meets their needs.

Building a better health system focused on the patient should start with these high-risk, super-utilizing patients. Building a system that cares well for the sickest patients with chronic illness, takes a full view of their health-impacting factors, and can drive improved outcomes benefits not only the sickest individuals but also everyone else.

A health system that can adapt to the intensity of needs, act proactively, and tailor interventions to the patient's unique profile is one that can deliver effective care. Matching diagnosis and treatment to the patient is the domain of medicine, but the people innovating in healthcare payment and delivery need to help encourage a more holistic understanding of the patient experience with care, to better connect the patient to medical knowledge and services.

\* \* \*

The snapshot of the highest-cost patients in the US indicates that much of the work to be done in chronic illness management must occur in the two primary government healthcare payment programs: Medicare (people 65+) and Medicaid (low income people).

But for the group in the middle, the employer-sponsored and private healthcare coverage system has an equally important job of helping the pre-Medicare people maintain good health so as to be as healthy as possible prior to gaining Medicare coverage. As heath is an investment, the mindset of segmenting these populations into their insurance category is deleterious to the idea that a person's health is longitudinal.

This is one of the key mindset shifts that must occur in a transition to proactive healthcare systems and longitudinal health.

The interesting part about this situation is that the same private companies often act as the payers in all three of these major health insurance programs. UnitedHealthcare has health plans in Medicaid, Medicare, and private insurance.

Aetna has the same—as do Cigna, Anthem, Blue Cross Blue Shield, and most other big names in healthcare.

These organizations and the healthcare industry as a whole segment people into cross-sectional categories that limit the view of the patient as continuous throughout their lives. A baby born into a low-income family on Medicaid may receive her first care through the Medicaid program, grow out of poverty and gain employer-sponsored commercial health insurance where she receives care and has a child of her own, and then as she reaches retirement age will transition from commercial insurance to the Medicare program where she has the option to select the traditional government FFS Medicare or to remain with an insurance company that contracts with the Medicare program through the Medicare Advantage program.

This woman has seen all three health insurance programs where the preventive services and care she receives early on will impact her health throughout her life. To her insurers and the health system, she is a part of three separate populations with her health data and records spread across many organizations. But to her, her life and health have been one and the same—no matter where she receives treatment or is covered for care. This specialization, fragmentation, and segmentation, just as was seen by Taylor with Unite Us, is not built for the patient.

In this scenario, it is possible that this woman received care from UnitedHealthcare through a Medicaid program, from UnitedHealthcare under an employer-based plan, and then finally from UnitedHealthcare again as a Medicare

Advantage plan. But from the system's perspective, her data and the incentives for investing in her care are not viewed as long-term despite the potential benefit for UnitedHealthcare. Paying for services and ensuring adequate delivery of those services to this woman as a Medicaid enrollee could have impacted spending during her time on Medicare.

As chronic illness is a lifelong affliction, it will become more and more important for the healthcare system to view a person's care longitudinally. As data and technology become more adopted and programs are developed to track patients' information over time, the ability to view health as a long-term investment is possible.[15]

Thus, the intersection of new payment models that generate incentives for this type of mindset and the promise of the Information Age bringing new digital health technologies to the field will allow the system to innovate and reform under these principles.

Driving investment in people's health across their lifespan is necessary to prevent the formation and exacerbation of chronic illness. Using payment incentives and new care delivery models powered by technology to do this is crucial to the goal of reducing the demand for health services driven by chronic illness.

As the book continues, this concept will be explored in more detail through payment reform and digital health technology innovations.

---

15    See Komodo Health

* * *

There are two challenges presented to the healthcare payment and delivery system under the precept of the chronic illness issue and the need for a more longitudinal view of health: 1) How can we prevent more diseases by addressing root-cause factors, and 2) We cannot prevent the formation of *all* chronic illness, so how can the system reorient to help manage these conditions?

The healthcare system is currently oriented to deal with those catastrophic and accidental issues. But now, we want to keep patients out of the system by helping them manage their chronic illnesses in their daily lives instead of just being there when things get out of control. We still want our physicians and hospitals to be there if something goes wrong because it will, but we also want to keep that from happening as much as possible. We want to manage our chronic conditions so we can live normal lives.

The system needs to help patients, like Morgan, to proactively manage her diabetes from home so that she can live her life outside the health system and to step in if there is a problem identified.

"Recently, I was able to use a patient portal where my DEX-COM (insulin pump) data can be uploaded to my endocrinologist. The endocrinologist looked at it, evaluated it, and send her changes through the patient portal. I just made the changes in my kitchen," Morgan described when I asked her how she prefers to receive care for her condition.

Morgan's point of view is personal and based on her lived experience. Many of the digital health innovators I speak with describe this type of mobile, technology-powered health system, but Morgan speaks from the impact these technologies have on her life. This is a small system designed in a way that works best for the patient, and these types of innovations are gaining popularity.

For the system to deliver care that is more effective and efficient, the use of technologies and new models that help patients manage conditions without the barriers, challenges, and issues can only benefit us all. This is the domain of healthcare payment and delivery innovation.

The CEO of CareMore Health, an emerging health company that has a different take on healthcare delivery, Sachin Jain MD, MBA, sums up this deep need nicely in a tweet:

*"The US healthcare system is primarily an inbound system. It needs to be an outbound system. #radicalcommonsense"*

The system needs to provide health with purpose—rather than waiting for sickness to walk through the doors—in a way that works best for patients.

## CHAPTER 4

# HEALTH DATA COLLECTION AND ACCESS

———

*The Economist* released an article titled, "The World's Most Valuable Resource is No Longer Oil, but Data."[16] Data is, of course, information on *us*. Our purchases, our demographic information, our incomes, our taxes, our app usage, the type of mobile device we have, our Internet use, and our favorite online shopping locations are all stored, analyzed, and sold.

When it comes to healthcare, having to write this chapter seems unfortunate to me in the technologically advanced society in which we live. Technology already does great things for our society and in our day-to-day lives. Behind the iPhone you see, or the app you use, there exists the

---

16  "The World's Most Valuable Resource Is No Longer Oil, but Data." The Economist. The Economist Newspaper.

extensive world of data. Long ago, data was collected using pen and paper and it took a human or an early machine to sort through the pages to aggregate and analyze the data. Today, data is accessible with the click of a button. And from data comes *information.*

Today, digital communication and information access are a given rather than something radical. My generation grew up in the world of the Internet and smartphones, so, naturally, we are natives of this digital environment [17].

You can order food from your mobile phone and have it at your door in thirty minutes, you can stream every movie ever made to your TV without having to leave your couch, you can send money around the world using an email address, you can buy stock shares in a company in Japan instantly, you can invest in the Euro from a beach in the Cayman Islands, you can buy a currency that is "mined" using computers from your cellphone and send it to someone to purchase goods and services, you can become famous around the world on social media without even leaving your bed, and you can see and live what is happening at the corner of Pennsylvania Avenue from your friend who is visiting Washington, DC for the weekend. We live in the information age where answers, images, and media can be found anywhere at any time.

So, why not in healthcare?

---

17   *Though I remember the time of floppy disks, the first desktop computers, and CD-based jeopardy on Windows*

* * *

In healthcare—despite the digital revolution having occurred in other industries like media, finance, and the movie industry—your primary care physician is unable to see what your endocrinologist prescribed you as a treatment. Your cardiologist is unable to see what your primary care doctor wrote in your chart about your health. Your week-long stay in the hospital with all the tests and information that is generated and stored in the hospital's electronic health record is not able to be used by your next office visit because they are often on different systems. Your physician and insurance company may still fax records to each other, just as your primary care physician may fax your medical history to a specialist. And one of the primary data sources for healthcare management and clinical interventions often has a month or more lag, so you can forget about real-time anything. There is no Uber Eats in healthcare.

What if the month or more data lag data is used to identify something important about your health, but is discovered two months too late? Next thing you know, you are in the emergency department and later admitted to the hospital because the drug your cardiologist prescribed stops working when the drug your endocrinologist prescribed is taken at the same time. This "quickly" was identified two months after it happened, but you are still sitting in a hospital bed very sick and costing a whole bunch of money.

In an industry where information literally saves or ends lives, the healthcare system has done a poor job of information management and access. Despite a whole generation growing up and utilizing the healthcare system in the midst of digital revolution, the healthcare system is far behind in widespread adoption of these technologies.

To better understand the innovations that are occurring and need to occur in the healthcare industry, it is important to understand the three primary "sets" of data and how they are used. Data, as I will argue, is one of the keys to flipping healthcare to a proactive system.

\* \* \*

First, there is clinical data; your medical records. This information is collected by physicians, nurses, techs, and other clinical providers. This is where your personal medical information is stored over time. Medicine has prioritized the medical record because your physician knows that the more information you can provide them for their diagnostic and treatment planning, the better job they can do. More data points generally equal more accurate predictions, answers, and treatments.

You probably remember the days when this information was literally kept in a paper chart by your primary care physician and a separate one kept by any specialists or hospitals you used. Hospitals used to store charts in massive stacks, much like a library. But today, your doctor can be found looking at a computer and clicking instead of using characteristically bad handwriting to scribble notes in your chart. With the Affordable Care Act came the promotion and widespread diffusion of the electronic health record (EHR/EMR). This was expected to be one of the biggest game-changers in healthcare. It was one of the most exciting things that came out of the ACA, and had long been discussed beforehand .

Unfortunately, the projected benefits were somewhat mitigated by the rapid market entry of many firms looking to fill the need for electronic health record software that was now mandated by the government. With this rapid market entry came different software packages and solutions, with different and incompatible coding and application programming interfaces (APIs). APIs create the capability for data to be shared and communicated between systems and databases. But despite challenges, fortunately, now the medical records of millions of patients nationwide are stored in electronic format just waiting to be leveraged to improve health. Is it? Well, sometimes, but on the whole, it is not.

Second, there is the lesser-known, but equally important, administrative data. This is the data set that is primarily managed by health insurance companies and other payors such as Medicare and state Medicaid programs. This data is derived from the claims that are submitted for reimbursement by your healthcare providers. It is provided in code form to indicate diagnosis, treatments, complications, and other services for which payment is requested.

At a basic level this can be best illustrated through the following example:

When you go to a primary care visit, they ask for your new insurance information and scan your card into their system. At the end of the visit, any tests or procedures that are done, as well as any screenings (questions you answer often on a piece of paper attached to a clipboard) and the visit itself are all reduced to alphanumeric codes and submitted to your insurance provider for payment. The annual visit code itself may deliver $100, the depression screening may bring in $5, the urine test done in-house may bring in $10, and the other annual tests may be included in the $100 visit payment. Everything has a pre-negotiated price or is otherwise covered by another payment. In the case of Medicare, rates are standardized by the US Centers for Medicare and Medicaid Services (CMS).

These codes all correspond with a procedure, diagnosis, treatment, or other complications. There are codes, such as the following ICD-10 codes for everything:[18]

X52 – Prolonged stay in a weightless environment.
Y93.84 – Injured while sleeping.
Z63.1 – Problems in relationship with in-laws.
V97.33 – Sucked into jet engine.

Or, more routinely, there are codes like E11.9, which is a code that can be used to indicate a diabetes diagnosis for reimbursement purposes.

These codes form the basis for the data the system uses to calculate economic information, prices, insurance premium rates, and are used for research to track diagnoses. Insurance companies often use them to perform care management for patients with significant illness such as diabetes, congestive heart failure, and other chronic diseases that often cost them a lot of money.

---

18 World Health Organization. (2004). ICD-10 : international statistical classification of diseases and related health problems : tenth revision, 2nd ed. World Health Organization.

The third major set of data is a loose assortment of socio-economic and demographic data, collected across federal and state agencies that is also available and sometimes used. This data is sometimes available in clinical EHR data. It is stored at a higher population-based level through census data and the American Community Survey (ACS). It is collected at the point of enrollment for social services, on your tax information, by local communities, and in-house at local social service organizations. I mention this because I recently published a paper about data collection at the point of enrollment for Medicaid benefits.

The clinical "medical record" data and the administrative "claims" data form the basis for the data upon which many healthcare decisions are made. The collection, storage, access, and analysis of this data is at the core of the healthcare system—no matter where you look. While the healthcare system collects and maintains a vast amount of data, it fails to use it to the level it should and to the level that is on par with data utilization in other industries, like financial services or retail.

Why? Well, there are a few reasons. Like any industry, there are many excellent examples of effective technology adoption by healthcare organizations. Organizations like Cleveland Clinic, Mayo Clinic, and other top healthcare organizations have taken to the new digital ecosystem more rapidly than most of the industry.

The reasons are numerous but chief among them is that this is *healthcare*. Healthcare deals with people's lives, and therefore any technology that is adopted must be seamless and extremely well-tested. One mistake and the extremely litigious environment that is healthcare becomes a major risk for organizations.

The next issue, and one that came up frequently in the work I did on accountable care organizations and high-risk care coordination for my thesis at Georgetown, is that technology is expensive. While healthcare is the single largest sector of the US gross domestic product (GDP), it is delivered by organizations that have very tight budgets and operations. Many hospitals operate at a loss, so capital expenditures into information technology in excess of what is required by law are difficult to justify. This issue is also relevant to physicians' practices that have even smaller budgets for this type of technology and whose tight workflows prevent the opportunity for unwanted complexities.

Not only is it difficult to justify, but there is not much evidence that these new systems or technology solutions are effective at producing benefits by way of quality health outcomes or cost reductions. The clinical evidence produced by health services' research has not gained sufficient conclusive evidence as to the benefits of many new digital information systems and digital health technologies. Research is expensive and these technologies are new.

Conceptually, they make a lot of sense, but there has not been enough research on a sufficient scale to draw firm conclusions. Thus, many of the gains in information technology adoption have been forced by government policy or adopted to improve efficiency, and therefore reduce cost rather than having a direct link to patient care outcomes.

But these technologies have potential and some of them are gaining an evidence base for success. With more time, research, and adoption, these technologies will improve to actually drive outcomes. Unfortunately, adoption has been slow and thus the cycle exists in which evidence is needed for adoption, but adoption is necessary for the evidence to exist.

Until recently, there has been very little incentive for organizations to adopt and invest in new information technologies because they still benefit from FFS volume revenue. Sick patients, after all, equal more revenue. But that is changing as new payment models build incentives to provide more effective healthcare services to patients.

Furthermore, when a physician needs to see a certain quota of patients a day for business viability, there requires a great deal of efficiency. Time equals money. Convincing a physician to take time to learn and implement a new information technology system is difficult.

Complicating the adoption issue further, the institution of medicine, and in particular the medical education system, has not instilled a strong affinity for information technology, digital health, and other technologies in new clinicians. Our new doctors spend years learning almost exclusively about the human body to be thrust into the health system— then are expected to manage and operate high-performance, high-revenue, and data-driven delivery organizations.

Healthcare is also big and administered through a variety of programs and organizations. There are just a lot of organizations requiring coordination. Independent practices, hospital systems, insurance companies, government programs, and other support organizations are all individual organizations that may or may not have relationships with each other, and therefore sharing information and coordinating processes that are best for patients is challenging and time-consuming.

This is where innovations like Unite Us and information exchange technologies can make a tremendous impact.

Beyond these core issues, the healthcare system has intensive regulatory barriers, issues with territorialism over data access ("this is my data, why should I give it to you"), a lack of technological expertise, and significant organizational inertia ("things have been done like this for years and I learned from the best").

\* \* \*

I argue that the major patient-level improvements to our healthcare system will happen in conjunction with and stem from improvements to these four areas concerning *information* derived from digital health technologies: collection, storage, exchange, and analysis. When it comes to transforming the healthcare system beyond buzz-words, the shifting of funds, and the high-level policy reforms, *information* is one of the keys.

When it comes to healthcare decisions, you hope your physician has all the information necessary to make an accurate diagnosis and an effective treatment recommendation. In a perfect system, your cardiologist will have access to both your endocrinologist's and primary care physician's records on you. But even in this perfect world, when it comes time to make a diagnosis and recommend a treatment, all that data is often still analyzed by a single person.

At your health insurance company, they receive all the information about your recent diagnoses, services utilized, and any treatments that occur through the claims data. Sometimes, this data becomes available to them months after the fact. Your insurance company has the incentive to ensure you receive necessary services and effective treatments in a timely fashion to prevent further deterioration, and, therefore, costs to them.

However, they are unable to act on the information in real-time. If you think about it, while health insurance companies have poor practices and are unnecessarily complicated, the incentive for them to improve your health does exist, but they are challenged by their remoteness from the actual point of service to the patient and their "information hands" are tied by the slow nature of their core claims data set.

Many insurance companies attempt to maintain a department that is staffed largely by registered nurses (RNs) to act upon the clinical-related information they receive through this administrative claims data. In this case, or care, management departments where they attempt to help their members remain healthy and away from the costly points of care like the emergency department, inpatient units, and specialists.

In many circumstances, these organizations are the only ones that receive all the information about your health-care because they are the ones that manage the payment.

In an ideal world, this information would be accessible by the patient, all their physicians, all their nurses, and even some family members in order to improve the care and accuracy of the recommendations made by health professionals.

Unfortunately, it doesn't work like that in most cases. Some companies and organizations perform better in this area than others, and there is a lot of innovation occurring to help solve this issue. Digitization and development of health information technology are rapidly accelerating, and the emerging changes to payment systems create the perfect intersection.

* * *

Kaiser Permanente is one of the most respected and well-known healthcare organizations in the country. If you live in one of their service areas, you may have heard their commercials or seen their advertisements emphasizing the word "thrive." With a strong presence in California and on the West Coast, Kaiser consistently receives the highest ratings for quality of care and outcomes out of any healthcare organization. It provides an example of the best practices in information sharing and access, and points to a way forward for the US health system. It is not perfect, but it is currently one of the best.

The Kaiser model exists in other health systems, but none on the scale achieved by Kaiser. Their 12.2 million members benefit from having their insurance company, hospital, and physicians operating as one integrated organization. As opposed to a separate insurance company, hospital, and primary care physician, Kaiser closely interweaves all three into one organization.

Besides financial and management benefits of having a vertically integrated healthcare payment-delivery system, Kaiser's information technology provides benefits that show the immediate way forward for the larger American health system upon which greater innovations can be built.

Kaiser, as a single organization, has access to all the data collected on its members in one system. When a Kaiser member goes to their primary care physician, the lab tests ordered by their Kaiser cardiologist can be performed. Both physicians then have access to the same information and test results, as well as treatments and medication lists. Everyone is on the same page and are able to work together to ensure more comprehensive care for their members.

In some locations, Kaiser offers dental care—something typically kept very separate from medical healthcare despite being an important part of a person's overall health. If a patient goes to their Kaiser dentist, they might also receive questions about medications prescribed by their cardiologist or get blood drawn because the Kaiser primary care physician suggested a cholesterol screening.

With this, Kaiser collects data at multiple points of contact with members, Kaiser stores data securely within the organization to protect privacy and to allow for easy access, Kaiser provides the information to the full range of medical professionals that provide services to an individual, and Kaiser has the ability to run any number of analyses on its data to identify patients needing extra support or to identify trends in the larger population that might affect the utilization of services in the future.

Right now, this is the gold standard for information collection, storage, exchange, and analysis in the US healthcare system. Kaiser is able to accomplish this because of its integrated, single organization design. It is able to build services around members because of more coordinated access to those members, at more frequent intervals than single-service organizations. This is not a full system redesign and innovations can go further than this model, but this is the best example that currently exists.

For most Americans, your dentist, primary care provider, hospital of choice, and any specialists do not communicate between one another unless there is a *very* good reason. Your primary care physician may collect clinical data and submit new claims into the administrative data once a year. Whereas at Kaiser, important health questions and screenings can, at a minimum, be obtained multiple times throughout the year by different providers.

* * *

Once again, our health system's ideal data and information technology strategy can be broken down into those four categories: collection, storage, exchange, and analysis.

When it comes to **collection**, frequent is better. The more data points that are available for use, the better when it comes to your health. If you get a cholesterol test once a year to test for an increase in your "bad cholesterol," you will be able to catch that deterioration in your health once a year. If you get tested four times a year for this common risk factor leading to heart disease, your physician's ability to detect and treat this deterioration is improved and caught sooner. This is an oversimplification, but this is the type of benefit that is possible from frequent health data collection at the point of the individual patient.

The problem with this is cost. Four cholesterol screenings are four times more expensive than one. But this is where one of the core mindset shifts: longitudinal views of health as an investment. Sometimes, it is more cost-effective to pay for more, less costly services to catch something early than to wait until larger expenses that later occur from hospitalization. Thus, health becomes an investment rather than an inevitable cost.

When it comes to **storage**, security and accessibility are important. People care deeply about the security of their personal health information (PHI). This sentiment is changing each day as health information technology provides new avenues and sharing of health data. This is also protected by federal law through regulations such as those in HIPAA and HITECH. These laws govern much of the organizational behavior surrounding health information exchange.

While the tenets under these federal regulations are expansive and detailed, these laws protect the personal health information (PHI) of all individuals with hefty penalties for organizations that misuse or fail to safeguard health information. If you have worked in healthcare, you are aware of HIPAA and the hours of compliance training you have sat through. In the health information technology space, one of the most common excuses for a lack of adoption of technology is, "Well, we have HIPAA concerns." This is one of the key regulatory inhibitors to enhanced information use in the industry.

Health data privacy is also one of the biggest threats to innovation using digital health technology. Google, Apple, Amazon, and other major companies looking to innovate using health data scares people. If the fears of data privacy discussion outmatch the voices for more beneficial technology, then we will stifle innovation and adoption. Privacy and protection of personal health data are important and should not be disregarded, but this conversation needs to be framed with regard to bigger innovation goals.

Google, Amazon, and Apple have tremendous capabilities and capital. If we can ensure the protection of personal health data, then funding these developments can only help. Privacy is a complex issue and likely merits an entire book.

Access to information is crucial, and thus the exchange of stored data is essential to the future of the health system. Ensuring the right people have the right information at the right time and place is the area where technology has the power to improve the delivery of healthcare to the patient, and may be the single most important place at which major improvement can be accomplished. Importantly, we have the ability to do this and now, as new payment incentives begin to diffuse the nation, it is likely that information access-providing technology adoption will also accelerate.

Beyond access, **analysis** of larger and larger data sets will usher in a new paradigm for medicine and healthcare payment and delivery systems. From big data used to predict the formation of disease in an individual to the identification of the most effective treatment option, the use of data and machine learning analytics to deliver on the promises of modern medicine will become the norm. Machine learning is also referred to as artificial intelligence.

When I talk about AI to people who are less familiar, I explain it as a method by which research and analysis can be democratized and applied to improve processes, outcomes, and our understanding of problems. Instead of having a researcher sitting at a computer running statistical programs, AI is able to do this automatically to draw conclusions from a vast amount of data in ways that a human is unable to or that takes far less time.

AI is fancy statistics that digest large amounts of data to automate the information generation process. It takes unintelligible data points and makes sense out of them for use by humans.

In healthcare payment and delivery, the automation of administrative processes, the connection of patients to the facility that is best for their condition, and the coordination of information across health service providers are just a few of the areas where enhanced analytic techniques will reduce cost and deliver efficient care to the patient.

In medicine, AI is currently and will continue to enhance and physician support and decision making. Do you want a single physician making your diagnosis based on the *hundreds* of cases they have seen during their career? Or do you want a computer, informed by physicians and research, to make a diagnosis based on *hundreds of thousands* of cases to determine which combination of treatments and data points will result in the best outcome for you? In statistics-speak, larger data sets result in better predictive power.

Small and gradual improvements to these four areas will be the catalyst for major healthcare system improvements. Right now, we are in a major expansion in these areas. The information age has just begun to enter into medicine, healthcare systems, and health policy. In healthcare, we are in the midst of a digital and technological revolution where the previously disparate systems and technologies are becoming smarter and more connected to enable truly amazing leaps forward.

Due to adoption barriers, it has been a slow process requiring support from other areas of innovations. But now, the intersection between payment and digital health information systems has provided a window for this type of change to occur.

Small, gradual improvements in technology and payment guided by new mindsets when it comes to looking at health will help the healthcare system support our nation's patients in their pursuit of wellness. These improvements are crucial to helping drive fundamental change in a system that makes poor use of vast amounts of data collected, and has been slow to adopt technology that can assist in leveraging existing data and collecting new ones.

# CHAPTER 5

# SINGING THE SAME OLD TUNE

———

The healthcare-academic community has been writing about and discussing these problems for years. Fee-for-service, the cost burden of chronic illness, the need for improved information exchange, failures of medical education to integrate physicians into the system's environment, healthcare's slow adoption of technology, and the "5 percent super-users."

Healthcare has a lot of problems and with every new election it becomes clear that, unsurprisingly, people really do care deeply about their health and wellbeing. At the same time, the national conversation about healthcare is often dominated by those sweeping efforts to solve all of healthcare's problems through the casting of ballots.

For a while, I was fully interested in large-scale system transformation at the national level. Restructuring entire industries and state health systems was very interesting to me. It still is, but I believe the approaches that are being used fail to achieve improvements at the patient level. Also, these conversations far too often ignore the importance of technologies in payment and delivery. It is too often that MRI machines and new drugs that take precedent over technologies that help with the interaction between system and patient.

For health policy and public health professionals, the conversation often gets dominated by the ways in which health insurance coverage is provided to the nation. Coverage for and access to healthcare services is the dominant topic in national health policy circles. Medicare-for-All, single-payer healthcare, ObamaCare, Medicaid Expansion, and The ACA are all major movements to provide health coverage to 100 percent of the national population. They give off the illusion that these solutions will solve cost and quality problems.

They may have an impact. But there are strong arguments on both sides of the coin. Instead of trying to solve the same problem with the same old solutions, perhaps it is time to try to look at things differently.

"It's the way we allow pharmaceutical companies to act."

"It's that we don't have universal healthcare like Canada or the UK."

"We need to pass Medicare-for-All, we need to regulate drug prices, we need to do this big thing. Let's write to our congressmen and tell them we pay too much for healthcare."

These are the narratives that get passed along in Washington, DC coffee shops, on Capitol Hill, and in households across the country.

Now, cost is an important consideration and there exists a great deal of fraud, waste, and abuse with our national healthcare dollars. This is a key area of focus for many individuals, but is beyond the scope of this book. Said briefly, we want to ensure that the tests and treatments provided to individuals are medically necessary and services are not duplicated. We want to ensure that people are not submitting false claims for payment when services are not rendered, and at a basic level, we want to ensure that our healthcare dollars are being used responsibly. We want to ensure that each additional test or procedure that is performed has a purpose and adds marginal value.

But the focus on cost and coverage alone ignores the fundamental goal of society's healthcare system. The conversation misses two points: when we try to solve all the issues at the national level with legislation, we often fail to reach the patient, and if 100 percent healthcare coverage is achieved but nothing is done to alter the ways in which care is delivered to patients (reactive rather than proactive), then the healthcare system will continue to operate in the same ways it has after all the other major healthcare reform efforts over the last fifty years. The point at which the patient receives care has not fundamentally changed, despite many alterations and coverage changes over that time.

A diabetic, now with coverage, may be able to see an endocrinologist or primary care physician due to the removal of financial barriers. But that patient will still receive coverage for four visits a year. If the condition gets out of control during the 361 days of the year that individual does not see a physician, then they will still end up in the emergency department with a $30,000 bill and a piece of paper telling the patient to follow-up with their primary care physician. Now, with coverage, the cost will still be felt by the system because the demand for health services has not yet been addressed. Underlying drivers of healthcare utilization—the diseases—have not been adequately addressed by the delivery models despite coverage.

Once again, it is relatively easy to fix prices and improve coverage should one have enough votes to do so. It is much more difficult, however, to actually improve the health of a population. But it is even more difficult to do so if we do nothing to change the way the patient meets the health system.

On a population level, once all individuals without reliable coverage obtain coverage, then there are likely to be some gains in health with reductions in utilization of emergency departments and inpatient hospitalizations (because previously uninsured individuals now have access to some form of primary care and preventive services). But once individuals without coverage catch up over time to individuals with coverage, the amount of improvement will reach a limit if the status quo is maintained by the delivery system.

Information gathered and time spent with patients during that now-covered once-a-year wellness visit is not sufficient to truly impact the health of patients. And we are still having patients get sick, seek care, rinse, and repeat.

Increasing health coverage from 90 percent to 100 percent will produce benefits, but these are giant projects to undertake—giant in the sense that they require an entire industry, country, and federal administration to make them happen. Large-scale reform, while it can show improvements and has before, does not accomplish the fundamental changes that are actually beneficial to improving health. That is, changes to the models through which we provide healthcare services to individuals.

Historically, in the US, we try to solve all of the healthcare problems through reshuffling and attempted sweeping reform at the national level driven by catchy sayings spread by grassroots efforts. When it comes to innovation, health policy has been playing the same games for many years, and much public investment has been poured into biomedical research i.e. medicine itself. Again, medical research is great. We all want cures and treatments for our diseases. But only relatively recently has investment into innovative payment and technologies aimed at the delivery of medical innovation to the individuals who need it begun to accelerate at a rapid enough pace, with an emphasis on information technology. This is one of the caveats to my argument about legislation— the allocation of funding to research and development under many of the large healthcare bills is beneficial to innovations that can affect patient-level changes.

\* \* \*

National scale healthcare reform—save cost regulation and improvements to health coverage—does not often trickle down to the patient level with reliability or significant consistency across the country. To prove my point, let's take a look at the Medicare program.

Medicare health coverage is accessible by everyone after the age of sixty-five (there are other groups eligible for coverage). Once you turn sixty-five, you will be able to receive Medicare coverage. This whole age group, for the most part, has healthcare coverage and access to healthcare services. But this does not solve the problem of keeping people healthy.

According to 2017 CMS data, 66 percent of people in traditional Medicare have two or more chronic illnesses.[19] This type of disease, which we know contributes to that 75 percent of healthcare spending, is very prevalent. Largely because of this issue, the Kaiser Family Foundation projects that per capita spending in Medicare will grow at an average annual rate of 5.1 percent over the next ten years due to a growing elder population, increased use of services and intensity of care, and rising prices.

Even in Medicare, where we see universal coverage, patient care services are still not producing desired outcomes, are inconsistent, and vary geographically. Chronic illnesses are still not managed to the extent of what is possible, and the delivery of healthcare services is still episodic and reactive.

To improve health outcomes, it required changes to clinical practice paradigms, models of service delivery, and innovation at the point where the patient meets the system. This is

---

19    CMS FFS Data 2015-2018

an independent function from coverage, though coverage is a necessary precursor.

* * *

We cannot keep singing the same old tune if we want to fundamentally improve the health system. The biggest disruptors in other industries have done so through innovating the locations and means by which data is collected, turned into actionable information, and shared with the goal of altering the experience and value provided to the end-customer. But it is all about solving problems or making improvements for the end-user.

I recently entered the market for a soup pot. Nothing fancy, I just needed a stove-safe container in which to cook soup because winter was right around the corner. Long ago, I would have blocked off time on my busy calendar to travel to the mall where I would find a Williams-Sonoma or Sears, in which I would peruse their selection of soup pots and identify one in my price point that I liked.

Two days ago, I went online to a popular e-commerce website and searched for "soup pot" and received all options that were available (all the options that may be available, period). Within five minutes, I found my pot, paid for it, and it arrive to my house just two days later. While I was at it, I also got some new bowls.

The retail industry, similar to healthcare, used to be made up of many individual and specialized outlets for consumer products. While retail does not have the same product as healthcare (i.e., people's lives and health), it is still a massive industry that has operated in much the same way until recently as it always had. That is, until Amazon.

Amazon simply started selling previously in-store items online, and offered to ship items straight to peoples' houses.

For the customer (or end-user), this saves time and, at scale, also saves customers money due to price competition between similar items on the website. During my search for a pot, I was able to complete in five minutes what would have taken me hours to complete prior to the explosion of e-commerce. In this, a single company was able to revolutionize the industry by solving a logistics problem.

They made it easier for people to obtain the items they want and need. While the creation and expansion of Amazon was by no means easy, the concept is deceptively simple and centered around the end-user. They solved a simple problem for their users and saved them time, provided incredible selection, and now dominate the retail industry.

Amazon first started shipping without their now-popular two-day shipping. They learned, halfway through their disruption of the retail industry that people still want to get things quickly, sometimes to the extent that the five to seven business-day shipping would not allow them to compete against their "you can have it now" brick-and-mortar competitors.

Adding two-day shipping addressed customer concerns and launched the company into retail domination.

Amazon illustrates the power of technology and design innovations for the end-user. More importantly, they solved a *time* problem for people. Time is a person's most valuable resource; Amazon saves people time.

While Amazon has grown into a diversified behemoth that is expanding into many different business models and industries, the innovation itself was the website that allows people to shop efficiently. It was a simple solution that drove massive changes to a powerful industry, one with a change-resistant historic operating model.

Healthcare is a powerful industry, also with a historic operating model that has been resistant to change. Solving problems for patients, reducing barriers to care, and enhancing the capabilities of physicians to produce benefits to patients is the name of the healthcare innovation game.

\* \* \*

The healthcare behemoth, UnitedHealth Group (UHG), parent company of UnitedHealthcare, grows larger each and every day with gains in membership and through start-up acquisition. UHG is number six on the Fortune 500 list. UHG owns about 630 companies. One of its subsidiaries, Optum, owns the third-largest Pharmacy Benefit Manager (PBM). Optum owns 292 companies, employs 50,000 physicians (more than any other healthcare organization), and continues to acquire and expand market share each and every day.

UHG and its activities represent overall trends in healthcare payment and delivery systems. In recent years, the trend in healthcare has been to horizontally integrate with previous competitors (e.g. merging between two hospitals in an area), to vertically integrate upstream and downstream (e.g. insurance companies buying hospitals), and to attempt to build programs onto existing entities that are already quite large in order to generate economies of scale.

While UHG is a commercial entity looking to maximize profit and value to shareholders, it is still in its best interest to reduce the cost of its insurance members. The discussion of ethics around their profitability and commodification of health, in general, is another topic that also deserves its own book.

In its pursuit of cost savings and effective solutions to sell to other areas of the healthcare industry through Optum, UHG has been acquiring innovative health technology companies. This is one of the ways that small, well-designed solutions can enter the larger health system and scale to benefit more patients.

An organization as large at UHG is unlikely to fundamentally alter its business model, especially since it is currently working so well. Traditional approaches of vertical and horizontal integration are their main mechanisms for maintaining market share, reducing costs, increasing revenues, and maintaining profitability.

Thus larger, more bureaucratic, higher organizational inertia organization is not likely to drive fundamental reform. However, the companies they acquire have the potential to drive impact in the larger organization by slowly but surely doing things better.

Companies like PatientsLikeMe, a social network for patients, and Vivify, a remote patient monitoring solution, were recently acquired by Optum. PatientsLikeMe utilizes social networks to collect data and gather valuable insights for research, to understand diseases, and to better deliver services to patients. Vivify uses mobile monitoring technology to monitor patient activity, vital signs, and other mobile-collected data to gather more data than what is possible at physician office visits—all from the patient's home

In theory, remote patient monitoring (RPM) interventions, like Vivify, can help reduce the number of patients headed to the emergency department and inpatient units because their condition deteriorated before intervention under the traditional care delivery model.

RPM companies are built around the idea that they can intervene earlier because they collect real-time data from the patient's daily life, when a patient might need less costly support, such as an in-person visit from a nurse to their home. Thus, intervening reactively, instead of waiting for patients to deteriorate and show up to costly points of care, is fundamental to the digital health technology promise of a better healthcare future.

Optum has reported that it will continue to push on with its new acquisitions and existing data to leverage advanced analytics and AI technology.

UHG, including Optum, a major healthcare institution itself, is not the answer to healthcare innovation and system transformation. But smaller companies and innovations that build a really well-designed product that solve a comparatively small but major problem for patients has the ability to be so effective that they might be adopted by one of the overriding healthcare behemoths that represent much of the healthcare payment and delivery system.

These small innovations can scale themselves, like Amazon, to disrupt a major industry, or they can be acquired or adopted by existing organizations because they add value and do something so much better. Companies like Vivify Health and PatientsLikeMe have gained success and adoption because they are well-built around the patient, leverage data and technology, and provide capabilities toward proactive management of chronic diseases.

Solving for patient problems, developing well-designed solutions, and building things that work will always gain adoption. While political pressures, the size of the problem, and institutional inertia are mountains to traverse, they are no match for well-built innovations. Disruption comes not from power or resources, but from solving problems so well that there is no choice but to adopt an innovation.

# PART 2

# CHAPTER 6

# THINKING DIFFERENTLY

———

Physicians are averse to change that threatens their identity and incomes, as we learned from Dan Skinner. Again, large organizations like UnitedHealthcare are massive and so ingrained in their operations that major change initiated from them is both unlikely and not incentivized. Sweeping federal legislation has the power to improve access to care and coverage, but has historically done little to alter the clinical models that deliver care to patients. Each time national legislation is passed, billions of dollars are shuffled around and reorganized with little effect on the ways in which healthcare meets the patient. Our health system reform efforts have been resting on moving impossible forces and pushing levers that fail to address the root cause of the problem.

There are a few mindset shifts that need to occur in healthcare and the ways we think about innovation and reform. Keeping in mind historical influences and growing chronic illness burdens on the nation, innovators need to look deeply at the needs of patients to identify and solve the problems and barriers to effective management and mitigation of risk factors for these conditions.

Many of our solutions have been developed from the system's point of view. It is time, then, to focus reform efforts on the experience of the patient.

We all suffer from the blindness caused by the tremendous institutional inertia of the healthcare system in which we are raised. From birth, we are raised in the healthcare delivery and payment models that now fail us. We teach students to think within the confines of "the box" in which we are all bound. We blame regulatory, payment, technological, and even patients themselves for why change has not occurred.

The current healthcare system is a work-around—a work-around that has adapted to outdated models, and one that has not been able to adopt new technology to enable the development of a system that actually works toward keeping the population healthy and out of medical facilities. To return to my prior analogy, it is a covered wagon that keeps being upgraded despite failures relative to the capabilities that we currently have. Technologies, payment model incentive changes, and philosophy changes have produced an environment wherein we are able to begin to upgrade the covered wagon in a way that slowly converts it from an upgrade-wagon on dirt road to a Tesla Model S on fresh pavement—all while it is still rolling along.

Only now are we in a position where technologies and payment innovations have been refined to the point that fundamental change can occur. But the way we think about health and the health system must first change, to seek out the ways in which these innovations can affect change at the patient level.

To see things differently, we must look at the system care for patients from the patient perspective.

* * *

I learned the failures of chronic illness care in the United States from an early age. I have been academically trained in healthcare management and policy at Georgetown University. I have also worked for organizations across the healthcare system—from clinical, to payment, to both policy and bio-medical research. I have talked to, learned from, and worked with people at the top of their field. I have sat in the room with top research institutions looking to fundamentally improve healthcare.

But no experience would have been able to prepare me for the most immersive, trying, and formative healthcare sys-tem education that is possible. My "bias" through which I view my work in health technology, health policy, and the healthcare field, in general, is firmly rooted in the patient's journey through the system.

To understand how, we must start at the beginning.

My first true experience with healthcare, outside of annual wellness visits to my pediatrician throughout childhood, occurred when I was twelve years old. As I recall it, one day relatively out of the blue, my mom began experiencing a great deal of pain in her side that she attributed to a kidney stone. And, just like that, our much-anticipated family trip to the beach that weekend was quickly derailed as my mom needed to go to the hospital for the pain. I was very young, optimistic, naive about the frailty of life, and very interested in having a fun week.

As a twelve-year-old, I was concerned that my mom did not feel well, but I had little to worry about because sometimes people go to the hospital. The next thing I knew, I was on my way to a friend's lake house in a very quick turn of events that I now know was orchestrated by my parents and their close friends. For me, that weekend was a new and exciting experience filled with boating and fun at a small lake across the Alabama-Georgia state line.

Upon returning home the following Monday, I had little idea that I would experience a moment that has been seared deep into my memory. So deep that I can, with little effort, transport myself to that moment to view it again with detail incomparable to most others.

I don't remember the exact words that were said as I sat in the passenger seat of my mom's blue Chrysler Pacifica. It went something like, "I was diagnosed with a disease called Chronic Myeloid Leukemia. But it can be treated with two pills a day and things are under control."

My mom, with her steady, bold confidence had just told me she was diagnosed with cancer. My mom, famous for her work ethic, upbeat personality, and unwavering optimism spoke of her diagnosis with the grace of a mother protecting her child, but also with an air of uncharacteristic uncertainty.

I remember holding back tears and having a surprisingly clear understanding of the situation for a twelve-year-old.

I will never forget the deep, sinking feeling and the dryness and stillness of the air in the passenger side of her blue Chrysler Pacifica.

That visceral feeling hardly went away in the years after, even if sometimes it was too easy to forget that my mom was truly and dangerously sick.

\* \* \*

Chronic Myeloid Leukemia, or CML, is a cancer of the body's white blood cells. It is considered chronic because the progression of this form of the disease can often take years to cause the type of problem often associated with cancer like leukemia—that is, hospitalizations, a mess of IVs, and a great deal of suffering.

When under control and minus any side effects from oral "anti-cancer" drugs, people can physically live their lives in a relatively normal way. However, as with any leukemia, the disease can quickly get out of control with "bad" white blood cells multiplying uncontrollably in a patient's blood. This state, known as blast crisis, is extremely dangerous and life-threatening. Much like other cancers, when untreated, this disease is that of uncontrolled cell growth in the blood that crowds out oxygen-carrying red blood cells and drains the body of the nutrients and oxygen needed to support life.

CML, thanks to some revolutionary science, is a disease that is often manageable with two pills a day from a class of drugs known as tyrosine kinase inhibitors (TKIs). Novartis brought the first drug to the market in 2001, called Gleevac. Thanks to this medicine, CML five-year survival rates went from 31 percent in 1993 to 59 percent during the period from 2003 to 2009.[20] Since 2001, there are now several drugs on the market to treat CML providing a decent safety net for patients and options to alter treatment plans if necessary. Most importantly, new drugs provide hope for patients and their families—hope against the ever-present risk of deterioration.

A great deal of biomedical research went into these revolutionary small molecule drugs. With great fortune, these drugs allowed my mom to continue teaching fifth grade, running races, and living a normal life—thus contributing to an illusion of safety.

Her care during this time required that she take these two drugs, one in the morning and one in the evening, and that she go to a physician's appointment once a month for monitoring of key blood tests that indicate the control or progression of the condition. Outside of the occasional appointment and the religious taking of her daily pills, it would have been an invisible illness to most. This model and disease archetype is consistent with many of the other chronic illnesses that have been discussed previously.

CML is cancer, and therefore is a chronic illness. Some cancers progress quickly, like pancreatic cancer. Some cancers, like CML, may take longer to progress to a stage in which they become evident. But thanks to the work done through research, for many patients, CML has become a chronic condition they

---

20  *"Leukemia - Chronic Myeloid - CML: Statistics | Cancer.Net". Archived from the original on 12 November 2014.*

must manage every day, but that can be kept in a stable position. This doesn't mean this is easy physically or emotionally, but this means that people are not confined long-term to an inpatient unit in a hospital. The standard of care for this condition allows people to live in their homes, and, assuming their condition is managed in remission by the treatment and save any significant side effects, they can lead a normal life.

During this time, it was very easy to forget that my mom was a cancer patient with one of the worst and all-consuming diseases out there—Leukemia.

\* \* \*

I was thankfully able to live a normal high school life with my mom as my biggest cheerleader. Post high school, I was able to get settled into Wake Forest University for my freshman year of school with the goal of becoming a physician. I was well on my way to meet that goal. After an excellent freshman year of undergraduate studies, I decided that I wanted to transfer to Georgetown University to supplement my pre-medical studies with a degree in healthcare management and policy.

Thus, I began my second year of school at Georgetown with a big move to Washington, DC. It did not take long for me to discover that health policy and healthcare management was a previously untapped field of study for me, and a whole new world became accessible—one that would captivate my attention and interest, and one where I have no doubt I will be spending the entirety of my life looking to improve and to understand.

As I began learning about the healthcare delivery system and its role in the delivery of medical knowledge to patients, I began to apply that learning to my mom's situation.

My mom's disease was discovered and brought under control quickly. This acute episode of care was handled well by the health system, as it functioned perfectly in the way it was designed. Her lab results indicating the rapid progression of her condition were quickly brought back into the normal range, and she was able to be sent home with those two pills a day.

Like many other people with the whole spectrum of chronic illness, she was left to manage the day-to-day needs of her condition on her own. As my mom was sent home with little support or the safety nets provided by the health system outside of her once every one-to-three-month appointments where clinical data would be collected in the form of questions, exams, and diagnostic tests. She, like many other patients with chronic illness, had to self-manage her conditions to the best of her ability relying on little data, information, or support from healthcare systems.

* * *

### DESIGNING AROUND THE PATIENT

The first key mindset and philosophy change that must occur in the way we talk about healthcare reform and innovation is where we look to solve problems. It is necessary to affect change at the patient level, and thus innovations and reform must be *designed around the patient.*

The patient's experience with a chronic illness is that of uncertainty, office visits, and often unanswered questions. For patients who know where to access reliable information written at an accessible level, engagement with care and self-management comes easier but is often done independently.

Patients are counseled by physicians for a short amount of time (fee-for-service pressures organizations to shorten visits to fit in more revenue-generating patient visits), sent home with a prescription, and left to manage their disease without much support.

For patients with a chronic illness as deadly as my mom's CML, visits are more frequent. For patients with diabetes, it can be more like every three months or four times a year. These office visits may last only fifteen minutes and this time represents one of the few opportunities for the system to understand a patient's unique barriers to care, self-management challenges, and to educate the patient.

The patient must deal with the uncertainty of disease, navigating the health system, and how to manage the condition. In this, the healthcare delivery system provides very little support, and has little ability to reach into the patient's home and life to provide a helping hand or to monitor the condition lest it get out of control.

The patient experience with the health system and support received has a tremendous ability to impact the health of the individual and disease outcomes. We also know that the individual's activities when it comes to their disease management (i.e. taking their medications, following treatment plans, and limiting dangerous behaviors like smoking) and their challenges are often causal factors that affect the patients' outcomes from the disease.

To affect change in national healthcare indicators of cost and quality, change must first occur in individual interactions between health system and patient. The treatments and research produced by biomedicine and biotechnology continue to produce new capabilities. The challenge for the system and the place in which the US system falls short, then, is how we connect patients with the knowledge and tools of medicine.

* * *

The UK spends about 50 percent less, in British pounds, per person per year—that's £2,892 on healthcare compared to £7,617 per person in the US. On a population level, the UK also has a longer life expectancy, which is often seen as an indicator of the quality of healthcare in a country. The US is at 78.8 and the UK is at 81.4 years. Recently, US life expectancy has also begun to go down to produce an even wider gap.

These differences are affected by many variables, but one of them is the quality of the health system in each country. The UK provides universal access to healthcare for permanent residents. In the US, on the other hand, there are millions of people without healthcare coverage and therefore without reliable, affordable access to health services. While this does not necessarily go far enough, patients without coverage are sicker than patients with coverage.

Access efforts in the US will likely help to affect this gap between countries like the UK and the US because access to affordable, quality healthcare is crucial to receiving any support from the health system. But once universal access to health insurance is established, the experience of the patient within the delivery system remains the same unless it is changed.

Had my mom not had excellent health insurance coverage provided by the State of Georgia due to her position as a teacher at a public school, and upon obtaining coverage under new coverage legislation, her experience with her care for her CML would be the same. She would still receive care at periodic intervals and be left to self-manage her condition at home with the hope that nothing goes wrong between one appointment and the next.

Patients without my mom's education and support from her family also require more intensive support than she did. Patients who have difficulty following recommendations of care from their physicians, have difficulty reading instructions on medications, and do not understand the importance of certain restrictions are the individuals who must receive support from the health system.

This is the problem. Access and coverage issues are important and the improvement of access to basic care is known to improve health indicators like life expectancy, pre-term birth weights, maternal mortality, and other indicators of healthcare. But moving beyond access and coverage, for the health system to improve care for individuals with chronic illness in a fundamentally different way, it requires building solutions to solve patient problems.

# CHAPTER 7

# CHRONIC DISEASE DETERIORATION

———

I spent the early fall of my first semester at Georgetown meeting new people, building professional relationships, and learning about the world of healthcare management and policy. As is typical, many students looking at the healthcare field see themselves as physicians; I was no different.

Little did I know that this was the beginning of my journey into the little-known world of healthcare's "behind the scenes." There I realized that the world of healthcare payment and delivery systems, and, perhaps, the area through which our healthcare system can be disrupted. For me, it was more like catching the healthcare systems management and policy bug.

*And, at the very least, if you get anything out of this book, it will probably be a fair amount of well-placed concern that writing this book is how I spend my free time.*

At the time, I was getting settled into my new environment and area of interest. But this is when my mom's winding and circuitous healthcare system journey would truly begin.

It was early November, on a routine phone call with my grandpa, when I found out that the TKI drug my mom had been taking for the previous five years, the one that brought her CML into a deep level of remission (the stage of cancer where the disease is not detectable and for all intents and purposes the person is relatively cancer-free) had shown signs that it was losing efficacy.

Remission, for cancer families, is "the safety zone" where, at least for a moment, you feel as though things are "okay." The fear associated with each new lab test and symptom is placated by the data showing that the disease is under control.

But after years of complacency and no complications, that old feeling returned.

There are increasing levels of remission in CML, with each one proving a deeper level of control. I remember the joy we felt in my house the day that the news came back about my mom's disease reaching the deepest level of remission. As I stood by the window behind our kitchen table looking out into our at-this-point-deep-into-fall backyard, I remember feeling the weight fall from our collective shoulders even if just for that moment.

I thought back to this moment frequently during the months after that feeling of safety was robbed from us all on that cool

November night I spent standing on a brick campus path while on the phone.

Quickly, after my grandpa realized he had shared the information with me before I heard from my parents, I received a call from my mom with confirmation of the news. After a recent blood test at one of her appointments with her oncologist, she received the news that the blood test used to gauge the progression of the disease and level of remission had shown signs that the medication was no longer preventing the CML from progressing. There was no way of knowing when the drug began to lose efficacy, just that the data collected *from the most recent office visit* indicated this fact.

In her case, it meant that a new mutant form of the diseased cells became active. Each of the drugs in the TKI drug class has efficacy against certain genetic mutants of the CML cell. The friend she had in her long-time drug, Tasigna, was gone.

A new type of cancer cell was floating around, and that called for a new treatment.

* * *

Genetic technology has progressed exponentially over the last three decades. Medicine now has the ability to predict future disease risk from DNA code, alter genes, and insert new genes into human cells. At the first point of discovery, many early genetic researchers expounded the curative powers of genetic technology. Progress has been slower than initially expected, but our medical capabilities in the area of genetics have now opened a door to the inclusion of such information into patient medical records and access to data that enables more powerful predictions and the targeting of treatments to optimize the likelihood of success.

The technology is there for genetics-based medicine. The delivery and payment of and for the technology to the people who need it has, however, not been so successful. Many genetic tests are performed by a single laboratory at extremely high costs, but in my mom's case it was crucial to monitor the disease. The medical technology and knowledge within medical institutions are strong, but connecting patients with the right technology, treatments, and at the right time has not yet progressed to the same level.

During the call with my mom, the return of the same deep-seated fear I had felt the first time in her blue Chrysler Pacifica was followed by more concern that she was running out of new treatment options. The feeling was a rug being pulled from beneath me.

But this time, the news was quickly followed by an attempt to get more involved. After years of remission and years of my growing up alongside the disease, I was determined to apply my new understanding of oncologic medical care acquired from a new research job at the Lombardi Comprehensive Cancer Center at Georgetown.

I told my mom that it was time for her to pursue a higher level of care from the top of the institution of medicine. It was time to find not just a new oncologist, but an oncologist with a deep specialty in this condition and one more involved in active treatment research and development for the disease. After roughly an hour on the Internet, I was able to identify a world-renown expert in CML located at Emory University— fairly close to our home in the northwestern suburbs of Atlanta.

I quickly informed my mom, and she accepted the suggestion. My mom's existing oncologist identified the new genetic mutant of the cells and, with it, a new treatment option: Sprycel.

I returned home for winter break with my fears relatively placated due to the apparent success of Sprycel. All indications led us to believe that this drug was working and we were hopeful for another eight-plus years of success, replicating the experience we had with Tasigna.

At this point, she was okay except for a small cold over Christmas.

* * *

## LOOKING LONGITUDINALLY

This type of call or situation occurs frequently in chronic disease care—especially in cancer, where part of the treatment challenge comes from the cancer cells' ability to mutate and become resistant to the treatments. This can happen in other chronic conditions and treatments as well, but regardless of reason, these diseases can get out of control from a period of control. This often results in a minimum of more appointments, tests, and treatments and, at a maximum, it results in emergency department visits, inpatient stays, and other costly utilization.

The inadequate management or prevention of chronic illness is part of the problem associated with all the costs derived from chronic illness in the health system. The old model of healthcare delivery, or the episodic and reactive model, fails to support patients to manage or prevent these conditions from taking hold of their lives and well-being.

The reactive and episodic nature of the system is informed by tradition, organizational inertia, and fee-for-service incentives. This encourages a *transactional care delivery model* where a patient comes to an office, data is collected (blood, lab values, questions, physician exam, genetic test), and that snapshot along with limited historical data is combined to inform the physician's decision of diagnosis and treatment.

Indicators of both diagnosis and treatment are backed by clinical experience, clinical and biomedical research, and are often set as recommendations by professional organizations like the American Medical Association, the American College of Obstetricians and Gynecologists, and the American Society of Clinical Oncology.

The key point here is that the decisions and treatments presented to patients and their families are based on the data. In Morgan's case, much of her diabetes treatment is based on her blood glucose level and long-term indicators of her blood glucose control through a test that looks at the HbA1C protein.

These readouts could be a blood glucose level of 130 milligrams per deciliter and an HbA1C result showing 7 percent. Both indicate the disease's level of control. During a visit, other tests could be run like a check of foot sensitivity using a tuning fork (as diabetes can damage the nerves in the feet) or an annual eye exam. No matter the condition, all decisions are made by some amount of data that, right now, requires collecting and analysis at a physical location and relatively infrequently.

But what if we can collect more data, and do so more frequently? If we know that data is used to make decisions about diagnoses and treatments, would more not be better? Would investing in monitoring and data collection tools be merited in order to catch deterioration at the first moment it can be detected? What if we could predict it beforehand?

The current system views the patient and data collection within the four walls of a healthcare institution. But now, the technological capabilities exist to enable this process more efficiently and effectively than ever before.

The healthcare system needs to facilitate the collection of frequent longitudinal data sets linked to individuals. This must occur to facilitate information exchange at the point it is needed to ensure the patient receives the right care at the right time and place. *Increasingly, that place will become the home.*

My mom's care during the "healthy time period" was marked by occasional visits to her oncologist at our local hospital. These visits would consist of blood work to measure the indicators for her disease. Much like any other check-up, the physician would ask questions to be recorded in her record and would send her on her way back to her daily life.

But here is a good example of the data constraints that exist in our healthcare system. One cannot diagnose and treat what is unmeasured. The first issue is that we, as a system, do not make very good use of the existing data collected in the first place. There are plenty of examples of successful companies and organizations that do use data well, like Kaiser. But overall, data is not leveraged to its fullest extent possible and thus offers a major opportunity for innovation.

The next step, beyond using data that is already collected, is collecting new data to produce new information and doing so more frequently. Collecting new types of data and at more frequent intervals is crucial to this longitudinal health mindset shift.

In order to remain ahead of the disease, we need to use our understanding of the medicine and physiological processes (e.g. blood levels of genetic material, abnormal lab values, etc.), understanding of demographic, geographic, genetic, socioeconomic, and other data to monitor conditions and potential deterioration in real-time. The information *must* be generated from reliable data collected more frequently.

A physician needs to receive a notification when you are at risk for an emergency department visit for your asthma a month ahead of time. You and your physician need to be notified when your Apple Watch ECG data indicates that your epilepsy may cause a seizure soon. You and your physician need to be notified when your activity level, your home-based cholesterol test, medical history, blood pressure, Apple Watch ECG, and demographic information indicate that you are at risk for a heart attack in the next two months. Data collection about diseases, identifying risk factors, and acting to treat new developments before they get out of control is crucial to transforming the system.

Helping patients to understand, monitor, and self-manage their conditions through data collection and clinical models that support self-management proactively is a solution.

The key to this is the development and widespread adoption of technology. This has been a discounted dream for many years, but only now has the ability to incentivize the delivery organizations to adopt these types of technologies and information systems gained enough traction to accelerate the process. The two innovation streams of payment model reform and digital health tech are intersecting, and this type of change is more possible than ever before.

# CHAPTER 8

# A PATIENT TO MANY, A PERSON TO FEW

———

"I have this cough that hasn't gone away for a few weeks," said my mom while lying in bed; I listened to her lungs with my stethoscope. Having recently completed my EMT training, I was all too eager to demonstrate my new skills and insights to her, despite little concern about a common cold. We sat in the upstairs bedroom of my grandparents' Cape Cod-style home in Northern Delaware just a few days after Christmas.

"It's just a cold that I've had for a little while," she said.

"Well, maybe we should call and see if we can get you an appointment. You might have bronchitis or pneumonia. We don't want that to happen."

"I've been taking Mucinex. If it's not better by the time we get home, then I will go see someone," she said.

Eventually, the symptoms got a bit better at home, and we began to think nothing of it. It was a cold or some other respiratory illness that is common during the winter (especially for a fifth grade teacher) and has happened before without consequence.

But it turned out to be much, much more.

\* \* \*

As I left home for the start of my second semester at Georgetown, I had no idea that this would be the last time I would see my mom living the normal, healthy, and happy life we had come to enjoy. I vividly remember sitting in the passenger side of my first car, a silver Volkswagen Jetta, as my mom drove me to the Atlanta airport. I don't remember what was discussed, but as I exited the car at the curb of the departing flight drop-off, I was left with her two self-created, and now widely known, family mottos "don't suck" and "earn your beer."

I got back to Georgetown, where I jumped right back into my overloaded schedule of activities. I passed my national Emergency Medical Technician (EMT) certification tests. I packed in a full course load of healthcare management, supplemented with inorganic chemistry and human biology. I was working part-time for a clinical research project looking at non-pharmacologic geriatric hypertension interventions. I was also working part-time for a research group located in the Lombardi Comprehensive Cancer Center, focusing on experimental nanotechnology-based therapeutics and gene therapy in oncology. [21] I was busy but learning about healthcare from high-level policy to microscopic genes, which was right where I wanted to be. I was thriving and things were good.

Soon came February and Valentine's Day. As was now tradition, a big box arrived addressed to me. My mom, always my valentine, had sent banana bread as was common during my years away from home while in school. This year, though, having moved out of a shared bathroom situation and into my own bathroom, my Valentine's package also contained bathroom cleaning supplies—a not-so-subtle *suggestion* that cleaning my bathroom was now added to my schedule.

I will never forget the day I opened that package in my college dorm room. Just as the memory I have sitting in her blue Chrysler Pacific, I hold the moment in great detail. At the time, I had no idea it would be the last package I would receive from my mom before her CML would start its precipitous deterioration.

"I have this cough again that still hasn't gone away for a few weeks, but I am headed to Columbia, South Carolina, to see your sister for a football game," said my mom after I called her to let her know that I received the message about my bathroom loud and clear.

Things were going well for me, my sister was doing well in her first year of college, and my grandma was visiting during

---

21   Without a doubt, one of the coolest things I have ever worked on and may ever see

the trip to the University of South Carolina. I was busy with school and hardly even thought about my mom's CML, now that her recent appointment in mid-December had provided us with the information that Sprycel seemed to be working. According to her oncologist, the new mutant cell that was resistant to Tasigna was right in the sweet spot for Sprycel.

This news, right before Christmas, had been wonderful to hear.

So, we thought it was just a cold. It had been treated as a lingering respiratory illness, as is common during the winter months.

It began with a lingering cold and a visit first to an urgent care clinic, then to her primary care physician for an antibiotic, and then another visit to her primary care physician. After weeks of fighting what seemed like a few simple colds off and on, my mom went on a trip to visit my sister for parents' weekend during her freshman year in college at the University of South Carolina.

She returned even sicker and remained in bed for the day after returning.

* * *

## BREAKING DOWN BARRIERS FOR PATIENTS: REDUCING FRAGMENTATION

This is where it became clear to me that any healthcare system improvements must be accompanied by efforts to break down the siloed, fragmented organizations that collectively form the healthcare system.

Though I often simplify for clarity, our healthcare system is not a singular "system." It is actually a collection of many systems that fail to collaborate, share information, and coordinate efforts. This results in duplicated services, inefficiencies, failure to identify problems early, and decision making without all relevant information to treat people as a whole complex person rather than through the lens of a single set of diagnosis data or a single medical specialty. To her primary care physician, what my mom was experiencing was a common respiratory illness.

My mom saw an urgent care physician and her primary care physician separately. Each has access to their own information, is told what the patient thinks to tell them (I have a cough), and do not share information with each other. Everyone has been to medical appointments where they are asked to fill out the same information each time, answer the same questions, and act like a record player with each new physician or facility.

These independent physicians and healthcare delivery organizations are a problem when it comes to providing patients with support for their chronic illnesses. The system exists in this way largely because of the transactional, episodic orientation models of healthcare delivery driven by fee-for-service payment models, institutional inertia, and medicine's deep level of specialization. This design is *not* like this for the benefit of the patient or because it is the best way to do things.

Patients will utilize a hospital where the cardiologist, oncologist, and pulmonologist are all independent contractors who operate their own practices. The hospital system is independent of the primary care physician, the insurance company is its own organization, the diagnostic center lab is independent, the endocrinologist is separate from the internal medicine physician.

The system—or systems, rather—through which care is delivered and paid for does not view the patient holistically. Just as social support organizations like those connected by Unite Us were specialized and focused on single issues, the organizations and institutions that provide care to patients are also specialized and single-focused. The expansion of medical specialties and sub-specialties and our historic agglomeration of specialties into single organizations has created a fragmented, separated system of care.

For patients with chronic illness requiring continuous and interdisciplinary care, our organizations fail to provide services that reflect the complex needs of the individual patient. Patients experience their disease all at once. They take their medications at the same time, and they can only be in one place at a time. One disease can affect another disease, and one medication can affect another medication. Treatment for individuals with multiple conditions is accomplished separately, despite the experience of the diseases collectively.

Information exchange failures and the use of current care models designed to approach multiple co-occurring medical conditions due to this concept is one of the greatest failures of the healthcare system. In a field where information, test results, and time are variables, it is bewildering that this is how healthcare is delivered to the patients of this country.

We know that the highest risk patients who cost the most and have poor health outcomes are ones with complex, co-morbid conditions. We know that these patients may have congestive heart failure and diabetes, or they may have cancer and diabetes, or they may have heart disease and chronic obstructive pulmonary disease (COPD). But the system is designed to treat each of these conditions, without regard for the others.

* * *

This is one of the key areas where innovators need to look when designing solutions for patients. In many cases, the knowledge and capabilities to effectively treat and manage conditions exist, but rarely in the same locations at the same time. Technology can and will continue to improve this area. However, across the country, this type of information sharing is a major deficit for the healthcare delivery system and contributes heavily to the poor management of chronic illness.

As a patient, due to this inherent system limitation, this is why it is crucial to store and track your health records, medication lists, and to be well informed of your condition. The health system cannot, as it is currently, be relied upon to make informed decisions based on *all* the information needed.

This is, again, where technology and innovation will also lend a major hand.

Not only is information access and exchange necessary, but so is a willingness to engage across organizations and specialties. Medical specialization and the nature of organizations lend themselves to tunnel vision when it comes to the delivery of healthcare services. A well-designed system that looks to improve health and the management of chronic illness would encourage collaboration, data sharing, and interdisciplinary approaches.

The point at which my mom developed a cold would have likely been of more concern to her oncologist than her primary care physician, who was just looking for flu or bronchitis-like illness. My mom's condition affects her body's ability to fight common diseases due to the impact cancer has on her white blood cells. Thus, any infection or cold is a potential indication of a change in the control of her CML.

When she gets a cold, it is a cause for concern, not because a cold in itself is a cause for concern, but because she is also a cancer patient with a disease that can make a cold much more dangerous. A health system built around fragmented medical specialties and independent organizations that fail to share patient data is one that will fail to adequately manage the patients with multiple conditions.

Had my mom's primary care physician visit for a presumed cold been shared with her oncologist, or better yet, automatically flagged in an EHR system as an indication of the failure of her immune system due to the progression of her CML underlying, her cold-like symptoms could have been recognized sooner.

This is not to say that the underlying cancer change could have been prevented, but it highlights on of the core failures of our system and an opportunity for innovators and reformers to address efforts to transform the healthcare system look at the point of care delivery to the patient.

Specialization can be enhanced through adequate information exchange, automated analytics, and automation.

# CHAPTER 9.

# THE DAY I WILL NEVER FORGET

——

On a Monday morning, I was in the lab when I received the call which I'd lived in fear of for eight years of my life—the two pills a day had stopped working and my mom's CML had progressed to an acute illness requiring a trip to the hospital.

"Robert, your mom has been sick for a few days, and we think she has pneumonia. We are taking her to the emergency room."

My dad was on the phone with the news that my mom had been taken to the hospital for pneumonia, but I instantly knew that this meant that her immune system was not functioning properly enough to prevent this type of infection— her leukemia was out of control.

"You need to make sure they have an oncologist see her immediately. You need to call Dr. Schafer's office. He needs to meet her in the ER. This is not just pneumonia, it's her CML," I said, as I began to remove my lab coat, protective gown, and gloves in an absolute panic. I hung up the phone and told my colleague that I had to go.

"Is everything okay?" she asked.

"No, I have to leave. My mom is going to the hospital," I said as I walked out the door.

In complete shock, I found the walls spinning as I walked out of the lab and down the long hallway to retrieve my things to head home for the day. With my white lab coat in hand and located in the heart of one of the preeminent cancer research facilities in the country, I walked down the hall completely helpless and about 700 miles away from my family.

In tears, I informed my boss, a leader in genetic cancer research and the emerging field of oncology nano-medicine and gene therapy, that I needed to leave because my mom's CML had progressed to blast crisis and was far out of control.

Without any words necessary about the gravity of the problem, we both found ourselves in tears and in a moment of silence and interaction at the deepest levels of what it meant to be human. We were both working in the field for the same reason—to prevent these types of phone calls.

I walked out of the building, in shock. I had no idea what would happen, but I knew that it would not be good. As I left the New Research Building of the University Medical Center, I once again found myself in an "everything is spinning as I walk quickly" moment. I began walking aimlessly, and made it to a quad outside a small chapel in the middle of campus.

As I sat on a small brick wall, scared, alone, and with tears rolling down my face, I had little idea what the future would hold.

While I was sitting there, my mom was being transferred from the emergency department at one hospital to the Bone Marrow Transplant floor of Northside Hospital in Atlanta, Georgia.

* * *

I had little idea that the next six months of absolute struggle against an all-encompassing disease and the tumultuous journey through the health system would be the most unfortunate but best teacher to a young student of healthcare management and policy.

Looking back though, no amount of education in healthcare management and policy could have prepared me to help my mom navigate the complexities of multi-system illness care in the United States healthcare system. No amount of experience could have predicted the barriers and failures we overcame. It took problem-solving, teamwork, hours of phone calls and research, and a lot of mistakes to ensure my mom had the best shot at beating a disease that was already a challenge. Navigating the health system should not be another challenge, but rather a support. Unfortunately, our nation's patients must fight both the disease and the health system along their journey.

While my education and connections did not prepare me well, it did make the process easier overall compared to the experiences of many other people. It categorically should not take a degree in healthcare management and policy to navigate the health system. The complexity and lack of user-centered design are not only unhelpful when it comes to chronic disease management, but is also harmful.

As I stood beside my mom during her journey through most of the major organization types in the health system, I was able to apply my education to better understand the current state of the system and the ways in which innovators and reformers can drive impactful change by solving small but important problems faced by patients as they attempt to manage their conditions and navigate the system for care.

Simplifying the system for the patient, designing solutions to solve problems, and driving innovation under these concepts is necessary to push better performance in our healthcare system.

# CHAPTER 10

# THE INPATIENT JOURNEY

"So be prepared. She is in a special unit with tight controls, you have to wear a gown, and there is a process to get into the sealed Bone Marrow Transplant floor," said my dad, as we walked from the parking garage during our first of many trips through the hospital and up to her floor—a route that we would come to take hundreds of times.

My mom was admitted to the Bone Marrow Transplant (BMT) unit of Northside Hospital a week before I was planning on returning home for spring break. The BMT unit is the "inpatient home" for blood cancer patients, regardless of whether they are headed for a bone marrow transplant or other hospitalization. Patients arrive at the BMT unit in various states of disease with some patients entering a new immediately life-threatening acute phase of the disease, some patients in good health but starting the bone marrow transplant process, and some patients receiving some other inpatient-only therapies.

As I approached the doors to the BMT Unit at the end of a long hallway, I could see the "airlock" chamber that keeps the external environment out of the unit's air system to try and minimize infection risk. It is a hospital, so infection-causing microorganisms are everywhere—making the environment especially dangerous for any cancer patient.

We entered the air-lock room where we waited for the doors to close before cleaning our bags, washing our hands, and donning protective gowns, shoe covers, masks, and hairnets to protect the patients in the unit from the deadly pathogens we carry around with us from the outside world.

Once ready and clean, we would hit the button to open the interior door to enter the unit. Upon entering, I saw that the hall was a racetrack-like set-up. It was as if I had entered a flying saucer out of a sci-fi film. Patient rooms flanked the perimeter, with the hallway wrapping around in a big rectangle. It was hard to believe that almost every room was filled with a patient battling some stage of blood cancer.

In the center of the circle made by the hallway was the nurses' station—a low counter with desks behind it. There were family waiting rooms, conference rooms, and a snack room in the middle of the hallway.

We walked around the circle to the other side of the oval to my mom's room, which was located in the corner. I braced myself for the moment I would see her. We sanitized our hands as we opened the door and felt the rush of air pass as we released the room's positive pressure seal.

I entered the darkroom with my mom's hospital bed sitting directly in front of me. She was hooked up to at least ten IVs and pumps, with bags of various colors hanging from the pole specially designed to hold them.

As I walked into the room to greet my mom, I approached with caution and hesitation so as to not touch or move anything of importance. After moving on from the initial shock of the image, I moved past the mobile computer station that housed EPIC, or the hospital's electronic health record. Each patient room has a computer to allow for quick clinical data entry into the patients' medical records and the recording of the medical care provided.

My mom, still in pain from her swollen spleen driven by the excess of white blood cells in her body from the acceleration of the CML, was glad to see me but obviously anxious about her son seeing her in such a vulnerable and uncomfortable state.

After gaining a small but level amount of comfort in the room, we started to talk about how things were going. She had just started a five-day, aggressive chemotherapy to try and reduce the cancer cells in her body and to, hopefully, bring her back into remission. As with any chemotherapy, though, the treatment can often cause its own problems and can sometimes be worse than the disease.

Here, in this room, we sat. Not knowing the future. We had been told that we could be there for twelve weeks or more, so we braced ourselves for many hours on the BMT Unit, and, my Mom, for her new 24/7 home. For an active, fifth grade-teaching, Tough Mudder-running, and stir-crazy person, she had found her own personal hell full of discomfort, pain, loss of autonomy, nausea, and cabin fever.

We would take shifts in the hospital to make sure she did not have to be alone. We'd spend the night in the room and rotate through my dad, myself, and my grandma with occasional help from friends. One of us would take the day shift, the other the night.

I spent most of my time observing processes as I paced around the floor hundreds of times. I paced and paced—sometimes for most of the night. Part of me wanted to see the way healthcare was delivered day and night and part of me, I know now, was unable to handle the emotional toll from the events unfolding before me, and thus pacing and counting laps provided a small respite.

Information was at a premium. The physicians would rotate their weekly rounds in the hospital. We would see one physician in the practice once a day for a week. We would try to ensure someone was present for the daily five-to-ten-minute meeting with the physicians, but these occurred at irregular times. Then we would see the next physician in the rotation. We experienced many such cycles.

The monotonous environment took its toll on my mom. It took its toll on all of us as we strove to be supportive of the person going through the hospitalization. Even so, the unchanging and cyclical nature of life inside the BMT Unit was difficult.

For weeks, we would ride waves of positive and negative news, new symptoms, and the hope for discharge. The uncertainty of it all was a constant reminder of the precarious situation we were all living in.

But the inpatient journey provided one benefit. She was monitored 24/7 by well-trained healthcare professionals. While discharge was the goal, it was scary to lose access to medical knowledge, technologies, and treatments at a moment's notice.

Sending a patient home following a hospitalization is one of the most dangerous points in a patient's journey.

\* \* \*

Hospitalizations and "inpatient" health services are expensive. In fact, in an estimate done by the Agency for Healthcare Research and Quality (AHRQ) using the National Health Expenditure Data, hospital care is responsible for $0.39 of every dollar spent on healthcare services, or 39 percent of spending.[22]

Unplanned and preventable hospitalizations are most frequently proceeded by an emergency department visit or scheduled outpatient clinic appointment that results in abnormal findings. Emergency department visits and inpatient hospitalizations are expensive and attributable to chronic conditions that get out of control and cause a long-term deterioration in a patient's health status.

AHRQ defines these episodes of care as:

*Potentially preventable hospitalizations are admissions to a hospital for certain acute illnesses (e.g., dehydration) or*

---

22  Agency for Healthcare Research and Quality, Healthcare Cost and Utilization Project, State Inpatient Databases disparities analytic file, 2009

*worsening chronic conditions (e.g., diabetes) that might not have required hospitalization had these conditions been managed successfully by primary care providers in outpatient settings.*

These often occur because chronic conditions are not managed properly outside the four walls of the healthcare system's institutions. Once a patient's condition has deteriorated far enough to merit hospitalization, the goal often becomes keeping the patient alive and getting an out of control physiological process back into a normal range. Thus, time spent in the hospital is still spent on managing conditions and not on preventing the same occurrence from happening again.

For high-risk patients with chronic illness, these preventable episodes of care are major drivers of cost to the US healthcare system and bad outcomes. In a 2017 study of Medicare data, high-risk patients making up only 4 percent of the Medicare population accounted for 43.9 percent of total potentially preventable spending ($6,593 per person).[23] In the same study, high-cost nonelderly disabled persons accounted for 14.8 percent of potentially preventable spending ($3,421 per person), and the major complex chronic group for 11.2 percent ($3,327 per person).

These individuals have universal healthcare coverage from Medicare, but the failure here is the delivery systems' ability

---

23 Wammes, Joost Johan Godert, Philip J. van der Wees, Marit A.C. Tanke, Gert P. Westert, and Patrick P.T. Jeurissen. 2018. "Systematic Review of High-Cost Patients' Characteristics and Healthcare Utilisation." *BMJ Open* 8 (9): e023113.

to proactively and effectively manage these patients in order to prevent hospitalizations known to be preventable.

This trend is the reason why the health system needs innovations that encourage reorientation to a more proactive system with new models and delivery technologies. Hospitals need inpatient hospitalizations to stay in business. Their entire business model and existence are dependent on a demand for their beds and 24/7 nurse monitoring. But preventing these hospitalizations and emergency department visits are nevertheless possible.

We need hospitals in society because we will always have sick patients who require these services. Perhaps the goal is to shrink the sizes of the facilities and reduce the length of stay, due to lower demand driven by more effective and proactive clinical delivery models.

As attempts at new payment models that help the system move away from fee-for-service payment to delivery organizations gain popularity and adoption, the opportunity now exists to adopt new models that help to prevent these costly episodes of care responsible for a large percentage of healthcare spending.

By supporting patients to manage their conditions and through more frequent monitoring to catch problems before they occur, the system can step in with interventions *before* hospitalizations occur.

# PART 3

# CHAPTER 11

# PAYMENT AND INCENTIVE FAILURE

———

Professor Robin Goldenberg is an adjunct professor at Georgetown University and a Medicare healthcare consultant. As a physician, he is able to distill the healthcare system's deep complexities down to understandable form. His beloved class, Health Care in America, is popular even among students who study outside healthcare disciplines. From 2:00 PM to 4:30 PM on Friday afternoons, he captivates his class with a masterful mix of fascinating healthcare system information and memorable sayings.

"Ye who has the gold has the power," he espouses to his students. By this he means that in healthcare, payment and funding often dictate the behavior of the delivery system. Physicians will perform new screening tests when they get paid for them. Incentives to start using electronic health records leads to widespread adoption. If a hospital gets paid more when a patient is admitted overnight, then there will be many patients spending the night in the hospital. The ways and means by which the "gold" flows through the health system are responsible for much of the behavior and ways in which healthcare services are delivered to the patient.

Similarly, the Chief Operating Officer of Wellcare Health Plans of Georgia left us, after a summer of managed care health plan work, with "follow the money." While we like to believe that healthcare delivery is dictated by physicians who spend years studying how to treat disease and improve health, the truth is that much of the patient experience in the healthcare system is dictated by intricate and negotiated payment rates and methodologies between the healthcare delivery organizations and payment organizations.

This is a distinct function from the issues of access and insurance coverage. Providing coverage and deciding who pays for the coverage is one thing. Once coverage is obtained, the ways in which the money flows to the services and products that are supplied to patients as services is a web of complexity. But this is an area that receives a great deal of attention from health policymakers and healthcare system reform advocates.

For the purpose of this book, I will discuss a few innovations in this area though there are many methods and systems being tested across the country. Specifically, we will look at the area of the exchange of payments between the payor and the deliverer of health services. In this case, it could be a government program performing the payments i.e. Medicare or state Medicaid programs, or it could be a private insurance company. Both of these payors pay for the health services provided by physicians or hospitals for their beneficiaries, or members.

When it comes to healthcare innovation with the potential to make a big impact, there is more work being done than just the development of technology solutions. It is easy to think of computers, laboratories, and engineers when using the word innovation. But the opportunity to affect the patient experience with healthcare services exists in innovation in payment methods to alter provider behavior.

This is one of the core areas of improvement and innovation for the US healthcare system. That is, the alteration and improvement of the financial incentives that are utilized by this payor-delivery relationship. These payment innovations are often referred to as value-based payment (VBP), alternative payment models (APMs), or pay-for-performance (P4P).

Back in the early days of the health system, when medicine was able to provide only a limited set of services, a simple payment for each service, or treatment, provided to a patient was administratively reasonable and feasible. This is where the dominant payment methodology, Fee-for-Service (FFS) was born.

To recap this methodology, when a new procedure, diagnosis, drug, medical device, or diagnostic test is developed, a new billing code is created or an existing one is designated for that new product or service. Then, the various payors, providers, and companies negotiate or get assigned a rate to be applied to that product, treatment, or service. We have tens of thousands of codes used in various coding systems that have been adopted both in the US and internationally.

In the Fee-for-Service payment methodology, the provider of a service (e.g., a physician, hospital, etc.) is paid a contractually negotiated or pre-set rate for a service provided to a patient. The provider of the service submits the appropriate code to the patient's insurance and payment is *eventually* sent. FFS methodology incentivizes physicians and hospitals to schedule appointments and fill hospital beds. As we know, this is a problem where both the cost to and the health of patients is a concern.

If the goal of the healthcare system is to improve the health of patients and successfully manage diseases, then there is a fundamental misalignment between how we pay the providers of healthcare services in the country. Under this arrangement, it actually benefits the health system if patients stay sick.

Because of this fundamental issue in the payment and funding space, it is tough to work toward reorienting the healthcare system to keep people healthy, implement technologies that can help improve patient care, and redesign health delivery around the patient.

Current healthcare service models and ways in which we provide care services to patients with chronic illness cannot be changed, unless there is an incentive to do so.

Under FFS, if the system were to drop current models and try to support patients to remain healthy out of the system–to the extent that is possible with our current technologies—the system may no longer make any money, and therefore would not exist.

Fortunately, this has been a topic of discussion for many years, and there are innovators working to change FFS incentives to develop payment models that are starting to shift the focus from episodic sick care to care models that incentivize providers to keep patients healthy, out of the hospital, and in their communities.

## CHAPTER 12

# PAY-FOR-PERFORMANCE: INCENTIVIZING QUALITY SERVICES

There are many ways to design systems and incentives to produce a desired behavior. During the evolution of payment models in healthcare, pay-for-performance (P4P) or pay-for-quality (P4Q) quickly became buzz words. It sounds pretty good. We all want to pay for the best possible outcome, and we certainly want to pay for quality. The idea is that price represents value. And value is what we want to receive for our healthcare dollars spent.

P4Q or P4P payment systems come in many shapes and forms, ranging from extremely complex methodologies to FFS-like payments when a *desired* or particularly beneficial service is performed.

First, we will look at one of the simpler methods employed by health plans and payors to try and influence healthcare provider behavior. To better understand this payment method, we first need to look at a brief background on quality measurement in healthcare. Or, how we evaluate the performance of healthcare providers or delivery organizations.

The administrative claims data and electronic health record clinical data are the data sets used by organizations that measure the performance and quality of the services provided by healthcare organizations. We, as a system, want to know which physicians, hospitals, and health plans are better than others.

Organizations like the National Committee for Quality Assurance (NCQA) and the Joint Commission are national non-profit organizations that rate the quality of healthcare organizations. For health insurance companies, NCQA is the major accrediting body that scores their performance. For hospitals and many delivery organizations, the Joint Commission is the primary body that reviews and monitors their performance.

Using the claims and clinical data from these organizations, NCQA and the Joint Commission rate these organizations across hundreds of quality metrics, and provide accreditation levels and ratings by which these organizations can be compared based on their performance within these metrics.

Quality metrics are important parts of the healthcare system. They come in three main categories: structure, process, and outcome. Metrics are created through an evidence-based process that indicates that a certain factor (the concept being measured) has a positive effect on some health-related outcome.

One of the simplest examples is the annual primary care visit. We know that annual primary care visits, or check-ups, are good for health. Thus, NCQA is able to track the percent of a health plan's members who receive their annual physical through the claims data once the provider bills for the appointment code. One hundred percent of a health plan's members receiving a primary care visit annually is the optimal outcome, and thus would result in a higher rating if achieved.

Structure metrics are concepts like nurse staffing ratios (the number of nurses per patient), the number of hospital beds in a facility, and the presence or absence of certain departments. Structure measures are like an organization's "structure" and basic statistics. We know that when a nurse-to-patient staffing ratio is too low then that can be detrimental for a patient's health, thus we want the staffing ratio to be at an optimal point.

Process metrics are the most common. Process metrics can be thought of as "things we want to occur for patients." The annual primary care visit is a process measure, as are certain screenings like depression, ADHD, and alcohol use. Annual flu vaccinations, refilling important medications, and mammograms are also recommended clinical practices and, so, for specific populations, health plans are rated on the percentage of their members who receive these services during a calendar year or in the recommended time frame. We know that flu vaccinations keep people safe during flu season, so we want to ensure that as many people as possible receive them. The concepts being measured are based on clinical recommendations to physicians, based on years of research and clinical practice paradigms.

Outcome metrics are the gold standard for quality measurement. Outcomes are what we want to occur when a person interacts with the health system. The most basic outcome metric is the mortality rate. The mortality rate, put crudely, is the "death rate."

For hospitals and health insurance companies, the number of members/patients who die each year is monitored overall and for certain high-importance populations, such as deaths due to pregnancy (maternal mortality rate). Outcome measures also include looking at specific lab values like the HbA1C lab test for diabetics. If the HbA1C level for a patient is under a certain number, 7 percent, then that is considered "controlled" and results in a positive score for that organization. Outcomes metrics show the results that we want to see in the health system—positive condition control and patients who get better or maintain a certain health status.

These metrics are how performance of the health system is monitored at the organization and individual physician levels, and they rely on the same sources of data—clinical and administrative. Knowing these metrics are related to positive health outcomes and to the activities that we understand impact positive health outcomes, we generally want them to be good.

This is where one form of P4P, or P4Q, comes into play. At both levels of the healthcare payment and delivery system, organizations are incentivized financially to increase ratings on these quality metrics, and, in some cases, penalized if they fail to meet certain levels.

In the payor-physician relationship, the following example details the way this works:

Great Health is a health insurance company. Last year, they had poor ratings for members receiving important depression screening questionnaires during primary care visits. Only 10 percent of their members received a screening, when we want to see 100 percent. With pressure from leadership, the quality improvement and physician contracting department develop a P4Q strategy to try influencing primary care physicians in their network to provide these screenings and indicate them in the patient's medical record. To accomplish this, on top of the existing payments, they send out a letter to physician's offices indicating that for every depression screening provided to Great Health members, the physician will receive an extra $5 payment.

In this scenario, the health plan, Great Health, uses financial incentives to improve rates of depression screenings provided during primary care office visits. The physician gets $5 per each patient this is done for, the health plan gets better scores, and the patient receives an evidence-based service.

Many people argue that the depression screening should have been done by the physician without the need for the extra $5 because it is a recommended clinical practice by researchers, and thus if the physician was doing a comprehensive job, it would be done automatically. Unfortunately, the health system uses these strategies for a reason.

From the health plan's perspective, improving quality scores can result in more revenue and a better reputation, so the investment in this type of program is worthwhile and is known to work for influencing the way health services are delivered to the patient.

This method can be applied to any metric or service that is desired by the payor. Outcomes can be incentivized as well. While we want physicians to strive for better outcomes no matter what, health plans and policymakers know that "you get what you pay for."

This payment method is used in a few models like the patient-centered medical home (PCMH), managed care, and others as well. It is often referred to as a pay-for-quality or pay-for-performance.

# CHAPTER 13

# THE FIRST ATTEMPT AND A NEW HOPE

———

Elliott was just starting out in medical school when he developed an interest in "health equity." Equity—the term referring to the idea that everyone should have the same ability to attain wellness, and the field concerned with researching and intervening into the differences in healthcare services, outcomes, and health of different groups of people such as racial groups, ethnic groups, gender, sexual orientation, and other groups of typically marginalized people. Black mothers have worse rates of death due to childbirth than white mothers. Individuals who identify as LGBTQ+ have higher rates of HIV infection than other populations. Low-income individuals have more difficulty accessing health services than individuals of a higher income. The list goes on, and is driven by social inequities that also affect the ways in which individuals interact with healthcare services.

Elliott, as a young soon-to-be-physician, was interested in delivering higher quality services to lower-income individuals in the Medicaid population, but soon came to realize some important concepts inherent to the ways in which the health system connects patients to the diagnostic and treatment capabilities of medicine.

Elliott would spend a good deal of time using population-based data and building off of the work of previous researchers to look at the magnitude of the variation of health services across geographic regions. This variation told a story that has motivated reform efforts ever since. Elliott, and others, looking into geographic variation in medical services, found that the rates of certain procedures were not necessarily linked to a medical need for those procedures, but rather to the supply of medical services in an area. Areas with more specialists have more specialist-provided procedures. A patient who sees more specialists will receive more diagnostic tests.

After completing medical school and receiving funding to continue his work, this research continued to reveal important insights into the delivery of health services in the country. Elliott and his colleagues revealed not only that variation across the country is significant and that places with more health services provided more healthcare regardless of underlying need, but also that healthcare is not very good anywhere it is delivered. Simply providing health services does not necessarily lead to better outcomes.

Upon gleaning these insights from the data, Elliott realized that in his pursuit of better care for vulnerable and low-income populations, it would be necessary to understand and convince people that the care provided would be effective and wouldn't drive too much demand for health services without any benefits.

Elliott and his colleagues realized that in order to improve the delivery of care to low-income and vulnerable populations, they would have to take on payment reform. The incentives of fee-for-service payment were too strong to convince providers of care, policymakers, and healthcare organizations to improve both the quality and efficiency of the services provided to patients.

They needed, in short, to change the models and ways in which healthcare services meet the patient.

* * *

The world of health payment reform is complicated and contentious. Why? Because when changes happen to payments, someone loses money or fears losing money. In Washington DC, these changes get debated and lobbied for and against by the powerful industry organizations that dominate the health policy space.

Organizations like the American Hospital Association (AHA), American Medical Association (AMA), America's Health Insurance Plans (AHIP), the Pharmaceutical Research and Manufacturers of America (PhRMA), and the Biotechnology Innovation Organization (BIO) each spend millions of dollars lobbying congress, attempting to influence policy, and trying to convince voters that their mission and platform is best for the patient.

Each organization and industry has their own take on payment model changes. But overall, there has been a great deal of progress made in this area over time, with many models and methodologies tried and evaluated for efficacy. The one thing that they all have in common, however, is a shifting of risk.

Under FFS, the risk for the amount of money spent sits firmly in the payor's lap. If a physician wants to or feels the need to run a large number of tests for a patient, the paying organization is going to have to pay for those tests. There are systems in place—like prior authorization and a determination of medical necessity as well as monitoring of providers for unusual deviations from their peer groups—to help stop wasteful and unnecessary spending. But, in general, the risk for the amount of money spent sits with the payor.

## CAPITATION

One of the first major movements in the payment reform space was the concept of capitation. Capitation is a method by which the payor is able to shift the risk of higher costs onto the provider of the services. Payments are made from the payor to the provider, typically a physician practice, on a per-patient-per-month basis—no matter how many services are provided. To illustrate this point further, the following table, adapted from the American College of Physicians, shows an example of capitation rates:[24]

---

24   American College of Physicians

| Column 1 | Column 2 |
| --- | --- |
| Member/Patient's Age | Capitation Rate Per Member Per Month (PMPM) |
| 0-1 y.o. | $25 |
| 2-4 y.o. | $10 |
| 5-20 y.o. | $5 |
| >20 y.o. | $15 |

From this table, you can see that a primary care physician practice caring for a fifteen-year-old patient would receive $5 per month for this patient's healthcare, resulting in an annual revenue for that patient of $60 dollars, regardless of the number of services provided for that patient.

Different capitation rates are determined based on the number of services required for the typical patient in that age group. From the table, we can see that patients younger than one year of age are of higher risk to require, or are suggested to receive under clinical practice guidelines, more services than other age groups.

Intuitively, we know that newborns and infants require frequent checkups and services to make sure things are going well during the first year after birth. Thus, the capitation rate is higher to account for this additional cost and time provided by the physician.

There are variations on the capitation payment method that detail what services are covered under capitation, who is actually involved in the contract, and some other incentives related to quality scores and meeting certain goals. But the basic principle remains the same in that a set amount of money per patient assigned to a provider is paid at a certain interval (monthly or yearly).

For the payor, this provides predictability for costs, and places the risk for high utilization on the provider of the services. This is a common but unsophisticated model that works well for pediatrics where there is far less illness.

Capitation works well, but it also has negative incentives such as providing fewer services than might be necessary in order to save money. There is no incentive to go above and beyond. Quality is still measured and physicians are still monitored, but this payment method provides little motivation or upside to the physician who is paid under this model.

And primary care services are less costly to provide in the first place, so it does not provide significant benefits in terms of cost or reducing costly services. Hospitals are not often paid capitated rates, and thus, the high-cost burden of inpatient and emergency department stays are not necessarily affected by capitated payment models.

One area where successes have been seen with capitation is in government healthcare programs like Medicare and Medicaid. In an effort to curb FFS spending, Medicare and Medicaid have created Medicare Advantage and Medicaid Managed Care as methods to try and shift risk for health services onto other entities, and to reduce the FFS cost inflation.

Under these programs, government pools of money are paid to private insurance companies instead of directly going to pay claims submitted by providers. Now, these programs can operate like commercial insurance companies.

Medicare Advantage plans and Medicaid Managed Care plans are paid a per-member-per-month payment for each member they enroll in their plans. Now, the risk is on the health insurance company and government pools of money are spent in a predictable way. It is now on the health plans to manage provider networks, monitor quality, and try to reduce overall spending through care coordination, contracting, and new payment models.

This payor-side form of capitation is the best and most effective example of the model working to reduce costs. It is continuing to become the dominant model of healthcare payment in government programs.

## CHAPTER 14

# THE ACO MODEL

———

Capitation does not provide much motivation to fundamentally change the ways in which healthcare delivery organizations provide health services. Recognizing that we needed something better, Elliott and his colleagues became more interested in how payors can include more impactful locations of care such as the emergency department, inpatient services, and also create incentives for more effective delivery models.

After years of research, Elliott and his colleagues set out to conceptualize a new way of paying for healthcare services that might incentivize providers to think carefully about the amount of care provided, the total picture of patient care, and to try to improve the overall provision of healthcare services in terms of cost, quantity, and quality. Fundamentally changing the healthcare payment paradigm would be a challenge conceptually, the research would be challenging, and, politically, it would be a firestorm.

Research conducted by the team looked at Medicare data across the country to build the well-known healthcare resource, the Dartmouth Atlas. Research stemming from the geographic variation of healthcare services and additional research looking at care patterns surrounding individual physicians became well known by the health research community earning Elliott, and the team, a national platform to influence the large- and small-scale healthcare reform efforts.

At this point, Elliott was no longer just Elliott, but a champion of payment reform efforts and a healthcare "household name."

Today, Dr. Elliott Fisher's research is frequently taught in public health, healthcare management and policy, and other healthcare academic disciplines. But his work did not stop there: there was more to be done.

Elliott and his colleagues formulated a plan to test a new model of healthcare payment to fundamentally change the way care is delivered to patients. Naturally, based on research focused on the geographic variation, they attempted to group healthcare providers in certain geographic regions together to incentivize them toward better patient care in that area more effectively.

To do this, hospitals, physicians, and other medical delivery organizations would be placed under a **global payment model**. Under this model, a benchmark of the total cost is determined for the patients assigned to these organizations. If, in the past two years, the patients assigned to these facilities received $10 billion worth of care, the benchmark might be set at $10 billion with a specific growth rate capped at 3 percent for the next year.

Thus, the goal for these "loose organizations" of provider groups would be to remain under the total cost of $10.03 billion for all the care provided to the assigned patients in the next year. If the group of delivery organizations uses more care than $10.03 billion then they are responsible for that extra cost. The onus for the services provided is now on the people who are prescribing and providing the services thus, hypothetically, removing the incentive to provide more care that exists under the FFS payment model. The people who use the money essentially are now responsible for spending the money.

The issue after this was conceptualized is how to get organizations to participate in the new model. The sell is tough when asking organizations to participate in the new payment methodology because they are being asked to take more responsibility, perform new tasks, and run the risk of losing money. So, an incentive to participate was necessary.

The team conceived of a model that incentivized providers to opt-in to the new model. If the organizations spent under the goal of $10.03 billion—the desired outcome—then the organizations would be able to "share in the savings to Medicare." A rate of shared savings would be agreed upon and if the group of organizations was able to spend only $9 billion on care for all the patients served, then they would split the savings with Medicare based on the pre-determined rate.

Thus, for the delivery organizations, they would now have an incentive to improve efficiency of care for patients to try to reduce waste, increase the effectiveness of care provided, and prevent patients from returning to the hospital by investing in adequate follow-up and care management capabilities.

The concept makes great sense, and thus Dr. Fisher and the team conceptualized a model where the FFS incentives can be mitigated using the research they did on geographic variation in health services.

Soon after the publication of a paper in the *New England Journal of Medicine*, where Dr. Fisher and the team discovered that most patients receive care from the same group of physicians, they decided to change their model slightly. They chose to remove the geographic grouping of organizations and replace it with linking patients to their physicians as the means through which total costs can be calculated for the baseline number by which shared savings can be calculated.

The team knew they were on to something big. This model was one of the first conceived that may be able to incentivize wide-spread participation in a way that traditional capitation was unable to accomplish. There was now a financial upside for physicians to participate, if they could just keep patients healthier.

Now, there exists an interesting value proposition for healthcare managers to change their business model after decades.

\* \* \*

Elliott and the team knew they needed to get this into the right hands in Washington, DC. So, they wrote a paper for publication in the most influential health policy publication: *Health Affairs*. Thus, the "Extended Hospital Medical Staff Model" was born and set to be introduced to the DC health policy machine.

I am hardly one to be at a loss for words, but during my interview with Elliott, I found myself feeling the twinge of nervousness coupled with excitement and disbelief of the opportunity provided to me. Having spent years studying and eventually writing my thesis on healthcare payment reform, I was talking to the "George Washington" of healthcare payment reform. I was talking to the person who could have inspired my deep interest in the intersection between the relationship between medicine and the delivery of health services to patients.

I am not one to fawn over celebrities, but this was one of the few people who could result in this kind of effect.

"Thank you for taking my call. When you agreed to set this up, I told all my health policy friends that I could not even believe I was afforded the opportunity," I said during the conversation.

He laughed and shrugged off the praise.

The opportunity to hear the story of my favorite model in healthcare payment was truly an honor to discuss with its creator. As we continued the conversation, Elliott went on to discuss the steps that led to the surprisingly quick diffusion and acceptance of the model into major healthcare system reform efforts.

"Our next thoughts, after the *Health Affairs* paper was accepted, was, why not reach out to MedPAC and see if they were interested in a presentation?"

Besides a publication in *Health Affairs*, the next logical step in introducing the model to Medicare is a presentation to

MedPAC, the Medicare Payment and Access Commission, which is chartered by the US Congress to monitor and source reform efforts for the Medicare Program.

So, he continued, "We reached out to MedPAC and asked if they were interested in a presentation about a potential model. They were."

So, Elliott took the presentation to MedPAC and walked through the "Extended Hospital Medical Staff Model" with the people who have, arguably, the most influence over major changes to the Medicare program.

"After the meeting, Glenn Hackbarth, Chairman of MedPAC, came up to me and said, 'Elliott, you're a smart guy, but this is a really stupid name,'" he recalled jokingly.

"'Why don't you put accountable into the name; maybe accountable organizations?'" Elliott said as he recalled the conversation.

"Well, it should probably have 'care' in the name," Elliott added. "It was in this conversation that we completely changed the name and I realized that the *Health Affairs* paper was soon to be released, so I sent a message to the editor to ask that he change the title and add Accountable Care Organizations to the footnotes."

At that moment, Glenn Hackbarth and Elliott Fisher created the name that would provide hope for payment reform. The **Accountable Care Organization** was born.

"The next five years were spent refining the idea, and trying to get it into legislation."

After those five years of effort, the Congressional Budget Office (CBO), or the organization under the Executive Branch that "scores" difference legislation to predict the costs associated with implementation, decided to score the ACO model for possible inclusion in Medicare policy.

"After CBO scored a bunch of options, the ACO model was listed as saving money. After that, it was included in every single draft of the Affordable Care Act," Elliott said in a very matter-of-fact manner, but with pride of achievement just barely evident.

Since the passage of the ACA, the model of the Accountable Care Organization has been explored widely. It has been studied, most famously, in the Medicare Shared Savings Program (MSSP) and now in the Next Generation ACO Model—both out of CMMI, the Center for Medicare and Medicaid Innovation. The ACO model has also been used by private health insurance companies looking to innovate in payment reform. Most recently, efforts have been gaining strength and popularity in state Medicaid programs such as in Minnesota, Vermont, Massachusetts, and Oregon.

Government payors, state Medicaid programs, and private companies have taken this model and attempted to use it in order to save money and produce better outcomes.[25] It has

25  Longyear, Robert L. 2019. "Medicaid ACOs, Information Systems, and Transitioning from Reactive to Proactive Care." *Georgetown University Repository.*

also been adapted and tailored to specialists such as in the Oncology Care Model, where the goal of better care also exists. While the MSSP focused on primary care physicians, the model also has applicability to other more specific specialties.

Since 2010, 900 ACOs have been formed in the US.[26]

\* \* \*

Evaluating programs like the ACO for effectiveness is hard because of so many variables associated with success and difficulty in determining causality. Many studies have been done to evaluate the success of the program with mixed results. Some show success, some show little improvement to the costs and quality outcomes they are designed to effect.

In addition, the primary point of study for ACOs is the MSSP. Many ACOs have dropped out of the MSSP, failed, or gone back to FFS payment. Critics use some of the negative outcome evaluations and cite dropouts as reasons the model has failed.

But at the same time, many ACOs have been successful, continued in the program, and expanded their patient enrollment. The Centers for Medicare and Medicaid Services (CMS) has continued to extend the model and build new ones for evaluation.

Since 2010, more than forty-two program evaluations and studies have been done on ACOs, across both public and

---

26 Impact of Accountable Care Organizations on Utilization, Care, and Outcomes: A Systematic Review. Kaufman. 2019.

private payors. A large review of all forty-two studies done in 2019 provides the most comprehensive evidence of the early success of these programs.

The most consistent benefits associated with ACOs are reduced inpatient utilization, reduced emergency department utilization, and improvements in quality metrics that evaluate preventive services and chronic disease management.[27] Thus, most agree that successful ACOs are moving towards achieving the ultimate goals designed by Elliott.

This large systematic review shows the ACO model, overall, is effective at producing the desired goals of a more proactive healthcare system. The results are by no means a slam dunk, and are not quite at the level expected by Dr. Elliott Fisher.

But by and large, the evidence is beginning to show that the model *is* working and even working better in some cases. The incentives, while not quite achieving the sweeping successes hoped for by the team, have nevertheless changed the behavior of the delivery organizations. The ACOs that have differentiated themselves have adopted technologies and new models of care delivery that focus on keeping patients healthy, more frequently engaging with patients, and continue to drive innovation and exploration of new models.

As with any new model or organization, there is a level of failure and learning that must occur to achieve results. The ACO model requires a fundamental change in the ways in which healthcare services have been provided for hundreds of

---

27   Ibid.

years, thus it is expected that some organizations will figure it out and others will not be able to effectively break from organizational inertia.

The important thing to take away from this is that the payment model change has incentivized a great deal of innovation at the patient level via new technologies, models of care management, and new delivery models. While not universally effective yet, learning and development have been very useful in designing new models of ACOs and new ways in which care services can better be delivered to patients.

Later on in the conversation with Elliott I said, "I am writing this book about the intersection of digital health technology and payment innovations—I see them as going hand in hand in order to make more universal reform possible. Payment reform cannot work unless services become more effective, and I see technology lending a big hand."

"We have been disappointed in the results because the model did not reach the level of our initial expectations—we were really hopeful. Like you, we are starting to suspect that technology, care coordination, and such are going to be instrumental in achieving our initial hopes," Elliott responded.

Now that new payment models have begun to mature, diffuse into the market, and gain more acceptance, the time is ripe for digital health companies to prove effectiveness at improving patient outcomes. Once proven effective, the adoption of new technologies fueled by these changes in payment will give the healthcare industry the necessary push toward full disruption.

## CHAPTER 15

# CONNECTING PAYMENT AND TECHNOLOGY

—

Under the ACO model, there now exists a financial incentive to change the ways in which care is delivered to patients by hospitals, physicians, and other organizations. Studying the Medicare Shared Savings Model (and various other iterations of the concept) have led to improvements in the model for future studies and implementations.

Many ACOs in the MSSP and other payment markets have been successful at reducing costs, and have managed to provide significant shared savings. Moreover, the head of the Centers for Medicare and Medicaid Services just recently announced the continuation of the model.

Venture-backed companies continue to pop up to take advantage of the MSSP and other ACO-like payment models, using advanced analytics and better, more frequent care management functions to try to drive cost savings. These companies add physicians to their medical groups, where they optimize the practice management then help to provide centralized care management and care coordination to patients. These organizations use analytics on electronic health records and claims data to identify opportunities to improve patient care.

Companies like Privia Health, Evolent Health, Aledade, and Oak Street Health are trying to drive shared savings under the Medicare Shared Savings Program and other ACO-like programs in Medicare. Importantly, the change in these payment models, while being performed by venture and private equity-backed companies, is driving efforts to try and reduce waste, improve care management, and other functions that likely benefit patients.

The use of these payment model changes is important in an effort to shift the health system from a reactive to a proactive delivery model. The overarching lesson that can be learned from the ACO model is that it has the ability to impact the behavior of delivery organizations and individuals that operate within them, when compared to the FFS model. These companies and organizations must, and are, starting to change their activities to deliver care differently.

When you talk to ACO experts and people who operate delivery organizations that get paid under these risk-based contracts, they cite some major barriers that prevent realization of the kind of successes that were originally hypothesized by Dr. Fisher and the team.

The challenges of delivering effective care to patients under the existing reactive model still remain. It is difficult to get the right diagnoses and treatments to the right patient at a time in which that patient can most benefit. It is also difficult to prevent health deterioration and formation of chronic illness. This is where technology and more frequent data collection/analysis can enable better care delivery, now that incentives are aligned.

The most important lesson learned from these programs is that the widespread adoption of risk-based contracting, ACO-like models, and other similar payment changes has resulted in investment, innovations efforts, and research in ways through which better care can be delivered to patients that can produce results.

The ACO model is not complicated. It truly is a simple model that made a small change to the ways in which healthcare service providers are paid, thus altering the interaction between patient and system.

One of the leading organizations that helps to research, improve, and implement the ACO model is Leavitt Partners, a consulting and research firm that operates between policy and business. After attending several ACO break-out sessions at the Academy Health Annual Research Meeting, I reached out to David Muhelstien, the Chief Research Officer of Leavitt Partners for an interview after seeing his presentation on the current state of the ACO model.

David was nice enough to set up an interview to discuss challenges surrounding the implementation of the ACO model in various circumstances. David studied health services research and law, with a focus on the implementation of health policies.

"I was always interested in health payment reform and value-based care," he said at the beginning of our conversation.

"We certainly have that in common. So, what have you learned?"

"Take a look at the ACA. What does the ACA do? It is a mechanism to adjust the payment of care and how we have insurance. ACOs are the only thing in the ACA that directly effects change in the delivery of care. They use payment to effect delivery changes," he said—much to my satisfaction, as his statement aligns with the purpose of this book.

Leavitt Partners grew its work in the ACO space from initial monitoring and tracking to a survey and later to more quantitative analysis about performance.

"I wanted to be a doctor and practice as a physician. I was in pre-med classes and majored in philosophy. I started getting into medical ethics and end-of-life care, specifically, the financing for end-of-life care. This really opened my eyes to healthcare financing. The mid-2000s, this brought interest in the payment for healthcare services—and payment is huge," David explains.

During my conversation with David, besides learning about our similar paths to health policy and management from an initial interest in medicine, he outlined three specific areas that are the major barriers to the successful implementation of the ACO model.

"First," he said, "organizations that participate in ACO models, or other risk-based models, still receive some or most of their revenue from the FFS payment system. As an organization, it is terribly difficult to operationalize the functions necessary to drive shared savings—care management and enhanced technology—under the ACO model when you still have patients that are paid for based on the volume of care they receive."

"So, if you want to have half of your organization's patients coming back to your facility for more care and to fill your beds and half of your patients kept away, it makes it a challenge to standardize operations? Yeah, that makes sense," I said.

"Yes, that's right. There is a CFO dilemma that occurs when a certain percentage of revenue is still derived from FFS."

Second, David highlighted another key issue: the facility-based model of care we hold so dear. The ACO model, on the other hand, encourages organizations to provide care in homes to prevent patients from needing emergency department, inpatient, and other services that are costly and facility-based.

"Hospitals finance their operations through bonds. They figure out the best-reimbursed service lines, develop capacity, and try to fill that capacity in order to meet the obligations of their bond-based financing," David continued.

Under FFS, hospitals invest in facilities and space to meet demands for the care they provide. These facilities are costly and require bond-based financing. Hospitals must, then, meet the financial obligations under bond financing to continue to operate. When you try to shift from FFS, upon which these organizations have built their business models, it is tough and risky to accomplish.

Third, according to David, the mindset of healthcare managers is still primarily focused on the financial health of organizations.

"Nobody gets their name on the hospital for taking money out of the system. The incentives for promotion and career acceleration in the healthcare management industry are still tied to the ability to generate more revenue and growth."

The mindset for evaluating the performance of healthcare managers must change from growth to meeting the needs of the served population, and from succeeding at meeting the endpoints of new payment models.

Currently, healthcare managers are rewarded for growing their organization's revenue. Now, they must grow the revenue in a different manner, using different methods, and through the provision of adequate and effective services to the patients they serve.

"This is a fundamental business model shift. When system people talk about reform, it is about how the system needs to be replaced over time. The ACO Model is not incremental, this is a completely different business model," David said toward the end.

Truly, the ACO model is an immediate shift in incentives and the means by which organizations make money. By removing

FFS system incentives, ACO-like models force organizations to prioritize different things.

After analysis and writing my thesis (and in-line with David's list) it is clear to me that there is a fourth item to add to those provided by David.

Truthfully, the health system does not know how to deliver effective medical services to patients consistently. Managing and coordinating patient care is lacking in research, implementation, and the skills to truly improve the health of patients.

Shifting the business model from FFS to an ACO model is hard because it is hard to generate shared savings by improving patient health. We, as a health system, do not know how to improve the health of patients through consistently effective services for the population at-large.

The system knows how to fix the car once it blows a tire or breaks down, but keeping the cars out of the repair shop altogether has not been a part of the playbook until relatively recently.

In a more positive manner, Dr Elliott Fisher suggests that "We have given health systems a new way of making money."

This is true. The power of payment changes can result in the conformation of delivery systems to the new incentives. Truly, the ACO model gives organizations the opportunity to make money in a different way, but via a path to profit nonetheless.

This is where care management and care coordination are important. For patients with chronic illnesses who see multiple physicians, visit the office once every three months, and live their entire lives managing their condition, the system does not provide support or monitoring to help reduce their risk of deterioration. Deterioration, in this case, equals higher costs under the ACO model.

At the same time, the system, by and large, does not work to prevent the formation of these conditions in the first place (for example, through investment in health education, healthy behaviors, social programs, and other efforts that can help people live healthy lives prior to developing preventable conditions). If the ACO model is adopted on a universal level, then the incentives will also likely drive investment in these more basic but impactful public health functions.

Care management happens across the health system. It happens in health insurance companies operating in various markets, it happens through discharge planning for patients who are leaving the hospital, it happens via primary care physicians, and it happens in other organizations. Insurance companies and managed care companies are classic examples of care management activities being employed to reduce the cost of care. Insurers and payors are the logical places through which care management activities would originate—because they are at risk for the medical claims submitted by their member population, and because they have access to all the claims data for their members who may see multiple physicians that do not have access to all the data.

Now, though, under ACO models, hospitals and physician groups must utilize and develop best practices to improve the management of care to their patients, in order to improve their services and to reduce the risk of patients requiring emergency department and inpatient services.

Proving the necessity of this, Privia Health, Evolent Health, Aledade Health (all start-up ACOs), have built robust technology-driven care management capabilities to try and achieve the goals of the payment model. These companies, built almost entirely on value-based purchasing under the ACO model, have used analytics and care management to improve care delivery to their patients to produce shared savings in their assigned patient populations.

But, of course, this is hard. ACO-like payment models ask organizations to do the heretofore impossible. They ask that they improve the health of the populations they serve, or at least reduce the demand for health services because people no longer need them.

This is where technology has the ability to bridge the gap between the institution of medicine, delivery of health services, and new incentives offered by ACO-like models.

If you ask a physician about why their patients end up in the emergency room or hospitalized, they will likely say a few things:

1. "I can't control their behavior. Once they leave my office, it is on them to follow my recommendations."

2. "I have no idea that they received care from a cardiologist unless they tell me. I have no idea what was prescribed or what was done. It is hard to deliver care when there are a whole bunch of providers that offer different opinions and potentially dangerous treatments when done at the same time."

3. "I see this patient once a year. I cannot control what happens outside my office over a year. Their cholesterol was fine last year, but now it is higher. I don't know that until they come back."

Care management functions attempt to solve these commonly cited problems by physicians. At a very basic level, these physicians cite patient health behavior (i.e., eating habits, medication habits, lifestyle choices, smoking, and other behaviors that effect health), information access and coordination across providers, and having sufficient data to make informed recommendations.

Technology has the potential to bridge these gaps to help inform physicians and other human-based operations in the healthcare system. Technology has the ability to help patients self-manage their conditions, to collect clinical data in real-time, and to better communicate with their healthcare providers.

I asked both David and Elliott about the impact technology and mobile health solutions may have on the ACO model.

David responded: "There is major opportunism for technology. Anything that can reduce the need for human intervention. We currently use manual record exchanges. For pathology and radiology, to automate the reading of slides and X-ray images would be huge. Anything that takes people out of the system to reduce costs would be useful and effective."

In a similar vein, Elliott mentioned, "Mobile technologies are going to be very important to improving care for people. Building a longitudinal data set is crucial to providing care. Liberating the data to create longitudinal records is necessary."

As we reached the end of our conversation, Elliott made a point to add, "It is important to understand what is important to patients, especially for disadvantaged populations. Recognize that, with any treatment, there are probably five-to-ten outcomes that are specific to patients. These outcomes provide dimensions that are important to patients. Digital tools can support much more meaningful choices at the point of care that will lead to higher-value treatments for each patient.

"Value is individual," he concluded.

Technology has the ability to break down major barriers to care faced by people, and it has the ability to collect the data necessary to accurately diagnose and provide treatment options to patients in real-time, while effectiveness can be improved by advanced analytics. It is through these innovations that the ACO model will likely be able to realize the hypothesized cost savings and improvements to overall health.

# CHAPTER 16

# PAYMENT FOR PREVENTION

———

The last chapter specifically, and this book overall, are primarily focused on changing the orientation and behavior of healthcare delivery organizations using payment models that encourage better patient care. This relationship is usually initiated by the payor organizations looking to save money. While financial incentives are often the impetus for major changes to payment and to encourage investment, the ultimate goal is the reduction in patient health costs associated, primarily with the utilization of emergency departments, inpatient care, and specialists.

The focus on altering delivery organizations to provide better care to patients with chronic illness is because these patients are already sick, and, therefore, prone to deterioration if their conditions are mismanaged. Changing delivery systems—and, crucially, increasing coverage for preventive care—can also work to ensure that patients receive counseling and preventive treatments, to prevent the progression or development of a chronic condition. This is where the care provider is able to catch a potential risk factor early on in a patient's life and then to work on medical treatments, lifestyle changes, and behavior changes to try and mitigate the identified risk factor.

Risk factors are key to improving the health system. Using payment, data collected and analyzed through technology, and current best practices to identify and mitigate risk factors is the name of the game. Risk factors typically fall into categories—genetic factors, lifestyle and behavior factors, socioeconomic factors, and available health services are common risk factor categories.

To summarize what has already been covered:

Genetic factors are essentially a more precise form of a "family history," so if all your maternal line of women have had breast cancer, then you are also likely at risk for breast cancer. If identified by a physician, they may recommend more frequent mammography screenings and suggest that you frequently perform self-examinations of your breast tissue.

Lifestyle and behavior factors are individual. These are factors like diet, activity level, and treatment plan adherence. If your physician discovers that you eat that Trader Joe's Mac and Cheese for every meal, they will recommend that you add more fruits and vegetables to your diet. The choice of whether to do this ultimately comes down to the patient, and we know that trying to change entrenched behaviors is one of the most difficult tasks for the healthcare system. This area is viewed as the holy grail of health research goals.

What may surprise you is that health services have little impact on the actual development of chronic disease. Health services are helpful to diagnose, treat, and manage chronic illness once it begins, but the root cause is harder to solve. Which begs the question: what is this all about?

That's a good question.

The goal of incentivizing the health delivery system to reorient from reactive to proactive care is three-fold. First, we do want to improve the care for patients who are already sick. Second, we want to begin encouraging more effective use of methods delivered by the health system to prevent the formation of chronic illnesses. Third, we want to encourage investment in technologies and alternative approaches to improving the health of a population.

By changing these payment models and essentially making delivery organizations responsible for a defined group of patients, new innovative approaches to healthcare can be explored and implemented. Now that volume-driven revenue is often not the concern, we can start to rethink what we deem to be a "healthcare service." No longer is filling hospital beds and driving surgical volume the centerpiece of healthcare but, rather, care coordination, care management, mobile health tools, and investment in new models of care that promote health.

That brings me to the socioeconomic risk factors, and back to Unite Us.

Socioeconomic risk factors are becoming the hottest topic in health policy, payment, and delivery. The "social determinants of health" (SDOH) are on the agenda at all major conferences, meetings, and research investments. These factors are things like housing instability, food insecurity, education level, income, neighborhood, race, ethnicity, adverse childhood events, and other factors related to social status, income, and opportunity.

People are at higher risk for increased healthcare utilization and disease due to SDOH factors. Typically, this population is impoverished, primarily black, and live in dangerous parts of town with bad physical environmental living conditions that lead to safety fears. People in these social settings may work several jobs, be unable to afford childcare, fear not making their rent payment on time, live on inexpensive unhealthy foods, and are generally under significant amounts of stress.

These factors contribute to health disparities—the differences in health between distinct populations. This could be age groups (old or young), racial groups (black or white), geographic locations (rural or urban), or any segmentation that may show a difference in some output.[28]

As an example, one of the most heavily researched issues in health equity is maternal mortality disparities. In a *New York Times* article titled "Huge Racial Disparities Found in Deaths Related to Pregnancy," Roni Caryn Rabin explores research that shows major differences in pregnancy deaths segmented by racial groups.

---

28   Cockerham, William C, Bryant W Hamby, and Gabriela R Oates. 2014. "The Social Determinants of Chronic Disease." *Am J Prev Med* 52: 1–14.

Black, Native American, and Alaskan Native mothers are about **three times** more likely to die from pregnancy than white women. The article leverages research by Dr. Emily Peterson and her colleagues under a CDC program. The problem grows when you understand that **60 percent** of all pregnancy-related deaths can be prevented with better healthcare, communication and support, AND **access to stable housing, food, and reliable transportation.**

Maternal mortality, or pregnancy deaths, is a well-known indicator of the quality of health services and the health of a country. Some communities and groups in the US face maternal mortality rates that are worse than countries like Mexico, Cuba, Egypt, Fiji, Tajikistan, China, Russia, and Iran. As we often believe the US health system MUST be superior to other countries, I use this comparison to illustrate that, for some people, it works especially poorly. Coincidentally, the rising costs in the US healthcare system can be attributed to a failure to provide effective services to groups that see higher rates of disease, poorer outcomes, and, therefore, higher costs.

Those high-cost, super-utilizers of healthcare, again, are the 5 percent of patients responsible for over 50 percent of the healthcare spending on a national level. Said differently, 16 million people out of the 320 million population are responsible for roughly $1.75 trillion dollars of spending out of the $3.5 trillion dollars we spend on healthcare annually. Breaking this down further, those 16 million super-utilizer patients often fall into the following groups: 65+, cancer patients, heart disease patients, diabetic patients, and patients with multiple chronic conditions. Breaking this down even further, the characteristics of the most costly individuals in these groups are 65+, low income, and have multiple chronic conditions. This could be, for example, an homebound individual with diabetic complications, congestive heart failure, on both Medicare and Medicaid because they are 65+, and rely on only Social Security income with few assets. These are the oldest, poorest, and sickest in the country.

It all comes down to social factors and our country's prioritization of health services, rather than social services that drive a large portion of costs. Fee-for-service payment has resulted in more health services spending and utilization for diseases that result from diseases related to social determinants of health.

If you are poor, have two children, work two jobs that fail to provide enough income for rent and food, then health becomes a lesser focus. *Trying to survive is your priority.*

To further illustrate this point, the figure below is the classic depiction of psychological needs for individual people as researched and developed by Abraham Maslow.[29] Maslow's Hierarchy of Needs is simple to follow as each person must attain the lower level before moving to conquer the next, higher level. When an individual is worried about where they may lay their head at night, the food they cannot afford to eat, and safety, then health—which is usually placed in the second level from the bottom—is thus supremely difficult to achieve.

---

29  Motivation and personality. New York: Harper and Row. **Maslow**, A. H. (1987)

Figure 1: Maslow's Hierarchy of Needs

Fee-for-service payment has tricked us all into believing that *more* health services and *access to more* health services are necessary to improve the health of the population. Altering payment models, thus, does more than just affect the delivery of health services—it incentivizes investment in new programs and services that have the potential to drive big change at the root-cause level.

"So, basically, you guys solved healthcare," I said to Taylor early on in our interview. To recap, Taylor and his co-founders at Unite Us have used technology to efficiently improve the ability for social services (i.e. housing, food providers, job services, and homeless shelters) to work together themselves and to connect to healthcare delivery systems where there is significantly more capital available for investment.

With payment changes that incentivize delivery organizations to take a more active role in reducing healthcare costs, Unite Us is a technology that allows a healthcare provider to coordinate and "prescribe" social services for patients who may require that type of intervention. Instead of prescribing pills and procedures, providers of healthcare services will soon be able to prescribe and coordinate subsidized housing, delivered meals, and transportation to appointments. These interventions are likely to have a larger impact on cost and health outcomes for a patient with high social needs. More value may be obtained through interventions like this.

A homeless diabetic, for example, may now receive a referral to a subsidized housing apartment built in collaboration between a hospital, insurer, and a local housing agency for high-risk patients. This diabetic patient can now store insulin in a refrigerator, have the ability to store food, have a safe place to sleep at night, and can work on managing their costly and dangerous medical condition without focusing all energy on where to sleep at night and finding their next meal.

Now, instead of three hospitalizations a year costing $300K to the health system, this patient requires $20,000 in healthcare services and receives free rent at a cost of $1,000 a month, or $12,000 a year. Thus, the inpatient hospitalizations and ER visits that cost far more than the combined $32,000 a year are prevented.

Besides the better coordination and patient tracking provided by Unite Us, direct investment into housing and food programs are also becoming more popular under value-based or risk-based contracts such as the ACO model. In Medicaid ACOs—the primary focus of my research at Georgetown and the program responsible for a high number of patients with SDOH risk factors—delivery organizations are either required or incentivized to invest in programs that can effectively intervene in factors like food insecurity and housing instability.

Changing incentives in the payment system can also incentivize investments into programs that can work on the root cause of both chronic disease and the development of factors that impact the ability of individuals to manage existing chronic illnesses. Once incentives are changed, new models and research will lead to new areas of investment that produce the most value.

# PART 4

## CHAPTER 17

# TECHNOLOGY FOR PAYMENT AND DELIVERY

——

After a long in-patient stay, my mom was released from the BMT unit of the hospital. We were scared. This was the sickest person I had ever seen, and it was my mom.

My cousin Bridget, an ICU nurse who lives in Delaware, flew down to help transition my mom from the hospital into our home. We set up the downstairs bedroom of our suburban Atlanta home with a hospital bed. My mom had been looking forward to being home in her "own bed" upstairs after months in a negative pressure room and highly controlled environment, but it was easier to facilitate care and for her to get around in the guest bedroom downstairs.

At this point, my mom's previously chronic illness, CML, had progressed to an acute illness leading to significant deterioration in her health. She had gone through chemotherapy, lost her hair, lost significant weight, and, more importantly, lost her independence and agency. She had faced ups and downs, pain, nausea, fear, and the stress of not only her condition, but also the stress of knowing she was effecting the lives of many people. But she was being discharged, and we were hopeful.

Once home, she was fully reliant on family and friends to assist in performing her activities of daily living, to administer her sixteen-plus medications, and to transport her back and forth between the outpatient clinic and home on an almost daily basis. The constant forty-five-minute commute was challenging for all of us, and quite taxing for her. She required transportation in a wheelchair because walking long distances wasn't possible. This was full-time caregiver assistance.

She was discharged on a Friday, and had her first outpatient clinic appointment on Saturday. Moving my mom out of the house, into the car, and driving to the clinic—located just one building over from the hospital housing the Bone Marrow Transplant unit, and operated by the same physician practice—was a tremendous orchestration and burden on all involved, but especially on my mom. We arrived at the clinic for the first appointment at 8 AM. Despite the time, the journey, and the challenges before us, we were hopeful to be moving in the right direction.

But that's when I was first introduced to the failures of the US health system's adoption of technology, outside of my classrooms.

At this time, I was enrolled in a healthcare information systems course as a part of my program at Georgetown. We learned about electronic health records, informatics, and the need for more "interoperability" in the systems.

Interoperability is the concept of linking information systems and records across systems and organizations, so as to facilitate the exchange of information. I learned of the failures of interoperability on a national level when the two major electronic health record companies, Epic and Cerner, were unable to share records between systems, and thus many hospitals and delivery organizations are subsequently unable to share information. But I had no idea how important this was until I saw it firsthand.

We were taken back into the clinic where there were few exam rooms, but rather a large open floor plan with reclining chairs to allow for infusion therapy and the administration of intravenous medications, fluids, and blood products to patients. This clinic treated blood cancers, which require a large amount of treatment, so the back of the clinic was organized chaos: IVs, chairs, and patients crammed into small areas delineated only by curtains.

Nurses, physician assistants, and physicians moved around through the crowded floor to see patients, administer treatments, and organize care. These were many of the same people we met and received care from when my mom was hospitalized. This was the same physician practice that staffed the bone marrow transplant unit in the adjacent hospital.

As we waited to see the nurse after bloodwork was taken and to see if my mom would require any additional platelets, treatments, or medications, we hoped for the green light to leave because everything was going well. When the nurse arrived to discuss the bloodwork, she asked several questions I felt she should have already known. I assumed the nurse had reviewed my mom's months long-worth of inpatient records that were clearly recorded in the computer located in the hospital room.

I was wrong. The inpatient and outpatient electronic health record systems were not the same, and were not interoperable. The clinic, at this point, was flying blind on my mom's care. What if they needed to know she was discharged yesterday? What if they needed to know that she was in the ICU for a week? What if they needed to know she was found to be allergic to a commonly used medication? What if she required special care for a platelet infusion that was discovered in the hospital? What if they needed access to her prior seven years of medical records that tracked the progression of the chronic phase of her CML? They had none of that, despite it being stored electronically next door.

I was shocked, concerned, and in complete disbelief. My mom had been cared for by the same physicians for months in the hospital, but that same practice did not have access to her records in a simple way? For people working in healthcare, we like to joke that physicians, nurses, and healthcare professionals are the worst patients. I assure you, they make much more difficult caregivers when confronted with situations that should never exist.

The data necessary to facilitate the best care for my mom was reliant on technology, and that technology was not being used well.

\* \* \*

For the people who operate physician practices, hospitals, and other health delivery organizations, they learned how to do their jobs the way they have always done it and from the people who came before them. Now, with ACOs and other VBP arrangements, they must learn how to do new things, adopt new models, and innovate. Organizational inertia present in medicine also exists in healthcare management and policy professionals.

The statements that represent this inertia are like the following: "This is how we care for people with this disease," or, "we just call patients for their annual visit to make sure they come in because it is important," or, "I can't do anything once the patient is sent home." Unfortunately, we know that the current model does not go far enough.

The emerging field of "population health" strives to research, design, and implement programs that have the proven ability to improve the health of a specific population of people. ACO payment models rely on strategies like those used in "population health management" to generate reductions in emergency, inpatient, and specialist utilization by attempting to improve the management of chronic conditions.

From the delivery system's perspective, this is accomplished through activities like care coordination, care management, disease management, disease education, behavior and lifestyle change, and through the enhancement of the existing faculties of medicine prescribed to the patient. Support, coordination, and information sharing is the name of the game when it comes to care coordination.

For the ACOs that have been most successful and looking across them as a whole, there has been an increase in care coordination activities and use of information technology to conform to new payment models.

What has become clear, then, is that a level of data and information system use is necessary to facilitate effective care coordination and value-based payment programs. This requires technology adoption.

\* \* \*

Technology is the application of scientific knowledge for practical purposes, especially in industry.[30] This includes medical technology such as the genetic tests used to monitor my mom's CML disease state, surgical devices like hip implants, diagnostic equipment like CT scans, and medications such as TKIs like my mom's Tasigna and Sprycel. Medical technology receives billions in investment each year, from both private and public sources. Organizations like the National Institutes of Health funnel these billions of dollars into medical R&D each year.

Medical technology, however, for all its benefits and excitement, is only useful if it produces benefits to patient outcomes (i.e. people resultingly become healthier or happier). This

---

30  "Technology." *Merriam-Webster.com.* 2011. https://www.merriam-webster.com (8 May 2011)

requires that the technology and the information derived from said technology, or that the treatments are available, sharable, and accessible to those who need it.

Unfortunately, R&D is expensive, and quite often results in something that doesn't work or does not work as well as something that already exists. Imagine spending $500 million on the research and development of a new drug, only to have it studied in human clinical trials and perform worse than the current standard of treatment on the market.

Medical technology, new diagnostic equipment, and new treatments are great things. We all want cures and treatments for the conditions from which we suffer. However, when it comes to thinking about the societal impact of these technologies, they are often not very helpful for a number of reasons, but mostly because the payment and delivery systems fail to provide the technologies efficiently and consistently across populations.

Technology is great. Medical technology is the stuff that makes the news and gets everyone really excited, as it should. But when we look to reduce the overall cost of healthcare, we once again turn to the chronic diseases that cost the system the most money. We definitely want cures for diabetes, cancer, heart disease, and CML, but right now, we don't have them. We have treatment options and medical technology, but even then healthcare systems fail to adequately ensure that all patients that need the best treatment for their condition are able to get that. The problem here, once again, is the delivery of the knowledge and capabilities of the institution of medicine to the people who need it, in an efficient and effective manner.

The technology needed here—to *really* move the needle—is information and delivery-system technology that helps the health system connect the right patient to the right medical technology at the right time, and to improve the proactivity of this process outside the physical walls of the healthcare organization.

The problem we have isn't a failure to produce cures and treatments. Medicine and research continue to deliver new treatments and technologies every day. Rather, we have a system failure where patients, for numerous reasons, do not receive the care they need, when they need it, and how they need it.

Our system fails at information collection, exchange, and analysis. This is where tremendous advancements and application of digital health technology to the health system will drive tremendous results.

* * *

It wasn't until payment models began to change that the system had an incentive or reason to invest in these types of technologies. In order to encourage the adoption of electronic health records, the Department of Health and Human Services (HHS) had to heavily incentivize, and essentially force, organizations that accepted Medicare patients (i.e. most patients) to implement an EHR.

When the system was unconcerned with the health of populations (and it still largely is) and had no incentive to focus on models that keep patients out of the hospital, there was no reason to be *strategic* about health technology that could enable improvements to the delivery of care to patients because it simply was not business-critical.

The change in incentives from models like the ACO has forced managers of healthcare delivery organizations to invest in programs like care coordination, disease management, and other system-based approaches to improving patient health. To improve care coordination, disease management, behavior change, and other approaches aimed at actually improving the care of individuals with chronic illness from the point of the first diagnosis to an acute episode due to poor management, information is required.

Care and case management programs that help support patients in both navigating the health system and in managing their conditions require more advanced analytics and information technology, but they also represent early efforts to extend the reach of medicine into the patient's daily life. Next-generation care, case, and disease management programs will leverage advanced digital health technologies.

To enable effective delivery system reform catalyzed by sustainable payment model reform, it will require the ability to actually improve the health of the populations served.

To do that requires effective information collection, exchange, and analysis using new digital technologies that enhance the capabilities and reach of healthcare delivery organizations.

# CHAPTER 18

# DIGITAL HEALTH

---

After the first visit to the outpatient clinic, immediately after my mom's release from the hospital, we were introduced to the challenges of high-risk at home patient care. This is where patients and their caregivers are tasked with managing conditions, both chronic and acute, at home without the support of the health system.

We would attend the outpatient clinic, my mom would receive platelet infusions and other blood products as needed during the clinic visit, and we would receive any adjustments to her medications necessary to manage her several co-occurring conditions that had developed.

By now, my mom had made it through all but one of the tyrosine kinase inhibitors that are used to treat CML. We had reached the last hope for a medication treatment for her disease—the next step was preparing for a bone marrow transplant. For that, she needed to get stronger, her heart strength needed to improve, and this last medication needed to work. The last drug, Bosulif, is manufactured by Pfizer. It was added to the medication list prior to her discharge, and now was included among the many medications taken by my mom on a daily basis.

Caring for a high-risk patient outside of the four walls of the healthcare facility is tough work. We had to repeat the same functions and duties as the well-trained oncology nurses during her inpatient stay.

This is where the system fails to support, monitor, and intervene for patients outside the four walls of a healthcare institution and represents a significant opportunity for improvement.

* * *

During my mom's care journey, one of the most difficult challenges we faced was handling all the prescribed medications. Medications are often the cornerstone of medical treatment, and, for high-risk chronic patients, there are often many of them.

At the time, we were seeing a cardiologist, gastroenterologist, ophthalmologist (eye doctor), and her hematologist/oncologist on a regular basis. The problem is each of them prescribes their own medications, maintains their own electronic health record, and none of them talk to each other.

When it comes to medications—a lot can go wrong. Medications are powerful tools used to treat medical conditions, and they do so by altering some processes in the body. But when you alter a process in the body, it has effects that you hope to be beneficial by correcting whatever condition you are looking to treat.

Sometimes, though, these altered processes generate side effects and adverse events. We have all experienced this before—for example, when you take Benadryl for some itching, you also become lethargic. When you are on fifteen medications, though, those altered processes start to build up and not only result in side effects, but the medications also can start to actively work against each other.

The consequences of this are numerous. A medication can stop having the desired beneficial effect, side effects can become amplified, a dangerous interaction can occur in the body that does more harm than good, and anything else that might occur when you mix a bunch of chemicals that are not naturally supposed to be in the body. This concept is referred to in medicine as "poly-pharmacy," which is essentially taking a bunch of medications at the same time.

Medications are at the heart of medicine and its knowledge. We have already seen, during the discussion about chronic conditions, that many of the diseases that plague the US healthcare system are treated and managed through the use of medication. Morgan's diabetes, for example, is managed using insulin and other medications to help maintain blood sugar, just as my mom's CML was maintained with two pills a day during most of her experience with the disease prior to its progression. As a patient develops additional chronic conditions or complications, more medications are added to their regimen to treat the new symptoms. This is how poly-pharmacy becomes a problem.

* * *

At the same time, we also know that patients are very bad at taking their pills and following instructions. Who wouldn't have some trouble when they take four or five medications at different times throughout the day? This is a concept called medication adherence, or treatment plan compliance. It is a major issue in healthcare, estimated to cost upward of $300-$500 billion dollars annually due to deteriorations and poor outcomes from patient failure to comply with the instructions of their healthcare provider.

As more holistic views of healthcare services gain acceptance, it has become clear that it is not a patient's failure to comply with instructions, but rather the system's failure to support patients. Looking at the patient level, there are numerous barriers faced by patients when it comes to successfully following treatment plans.

Medication adherence and treatment plan noncompliance are also a reason that many people cite as to why value-based care is unable to work. Think again of: "We cannot control what happens when a patient leaves our offices or hospitals." This is the quote commonly heard from physicians and others who oppose payment reform because they don't believe it is possible to actually effect the level of improvement necessary in patients, largely because personal behavior and adherence issues.

During my mom's care journey, we created a medication calendar to ensure that she took each medication at the right time each day. This was very important to manage her symptoms, comfort, and help treat her conditions. But for any number of reasons, medication adherence is poor in the population and particularly in high-risk patients with multiple chronic conditions.

This leads to the development of complications, deterioration of a patient's condition, and ultimately to bad health outcomes. This also drives the cost up when patients get worse and have to go to the emergency room or get admitted to the hospital. Needless to say, the healthcare system wants people to take their medication, but doesn't do a good job of supporting them or recognizing when they do not do so until it is too late.

Not taking a medication can lead to deterioration that may not be caught until the patient shows up in the emergency department. This is a terrible cycle and is the heart of our system's failure.

* * *

During the interim period between graduation from Georgetown and a new job, I decided to try my hand at some freelance healthcare consulting for start-up companies because I wanted to gain experience in the digital health space, and I had some extra time on my hands.

After meeting the CEO of Montuno Software during a consulting project, he made me an offer to join the company. It was an opportunity to pursue an innovative digital solution that I could not refuse. Montuno Software is a start-up digital health technology company looking to revolutionize the management and treatment of chronic conditions by helping patients manage their medications. To me, it was where my interest in innovation and knowledge of health system failures could meet to work on a solution.

In a last-minute, late-night kinda deal, I signed the offer to join the company as director of product management. I jumped into a risky but promising company, with an app that already helps patients manage complex medication regimens and with sights set on a larger impact.

What does Montuno do? They have a technology platform that helps support patients, their families, and the health system in managing medication adherence. Patients have an app that has their medication list and instructions to remind them to take their pills, families can monitor one another remotely to make sure everyone is taking their medications, and healthcare providers can monitor their patients to step in if someone needs help via a real-time dashboard. The last part was what I was hired to develop, and then convince healthcare organizations to adopt.

The platform stores medication list data, and allows for management of small and large medication lists to make sure that dangerous drug interactions can be prevented, medication can be removed if it no longer becomes necessary, and a patient's health status and adherence can be tracked to make sure that everything is going well. If it is not, a professional can contact the patient via built-in telehealth tools to ensure that a solution is found or an intervention can be made.

This is digital, mobile engagement for care management programs in health insurers and ACOs. Now, patients receive a smartphone application to manage medications, and their history and health status can be shared with physicians and care managers in real-time, as opposed to the low-frequency ways in which it has always been done.

This type of solution fits into the heart of what this book is about and the area in which mobile health technology can make a big impact in terms of data. Data can now be collected in the patient's home, feeding it to the system to enhance the knowledge and existing capabilities, and to intervene in identified patient health issues before they end up in the emergency department, hospitalized, or otherwise requiring more intensive services.

With Montuno's platform, the healthcare system can monitor patients as they live their lives and step in when needed while providing an app that is useful and solves an important problem. This is an innovation built around the patient to solve patient issues.

Instead of waiting for a patient to get worse and show up at the ER or their physician's office, the system is able to shift to preventing that visit in the first place. Technology, like mobile apps and wearables, has advanced to the point where systems like Montuno can be built to generate real-time, real-patient information to help manage conditions and to inform interventions if something starts to go wrong.

\* \* \*

Combined with health policy's efforts to innovate using payment method changes, part two of the future of healthcare transformation is digital technology that enables more efficient and effective delivery of medicine's knowledge to patients at more frequent intervals.

Hundreds of start-ups and well-established technology companies are working to solve key problems that plague the system, providing hope for the future of healthcare payment and delivery but also for individual behavior change, social needs, and even policy.

I set out to write a book on healthcare system innovation. I knew that I was going to include a good deal of innovation in digital health technology in this book. Little did I know that I was going to have a front-row seat.

This type of technology and innovation is all about data and information that reduces barriers, informs care services, and predicts certain outcomes.

Information is key to drive the type of reform I'm talking about. If we are going to manage chronic conditions better and reorient the healthcare system to a proactive one, it will require that the right people have the right information at the right time and place. This is where technology will be able to drive significant benefits.

Technology in the field of "medicine" is also important. The MRI, DaVinci surgical robot, and all those neat flashy tools for doctors to play with are extremely important to providing knowledge and treatments. But we are talking about technology enabling healthcare payment and delivery innovation. That, while interdependent with medical technology, is a relatively new development for the field.

Working at Montuno provided me the opportunity to be part of solving problems faced by patients, every day. Through my role, I was able to inform the development of an innovative mobile product, build the business model, and interact with potential customers.

My work at Montuno was greatly informed by my research, formal education, and from firsthand experience at my mom's side during her care journey. I was able to learn from and work with the people who are trying to make technology a core feature in the US healthcare system, to extend and enhance the capabilities of medicine.

One of the benefits of digital health technology is its scalability and relatively inexpensive implementation costs when compared to brick and mortar and more "people-needing" innovations.

*But the place where digital health innovation truly shines is in its ability to collect, store, exchange, and analyze data to generate actionable information.*

In biomedical technology, the focus is precision and capability. The goal is to see deeper, diagnose more accurately using those precise measurements, and to generate new treatment capabilities that are new or better than those before.

But the application of technology to the actual payment for and delivery of those technologies and the more accurate matching of them to individuals is relatively new and will be a game-changer for the health system—if the challenges of clinical adoption, financing, and payment incentives can be conquered.

# CHAPTER 19

# TECHNOLOGY THAT COLLECTS

———

"Did someone give her the carvedilol?"

"How about the Bosulif?"

"Did someone take her blood pressure and what was it?"

"How was she feeling this morning?"

This is how the conversation usually began each morning as my multiple family members shared the activities of caregiving each day.

These questions were discussed on a daily basis. We were well-prepared, skilled, and advised either ourselves or through help from others when it came to clinical care, personal care, and the navigation of the health system. But it was tough to manage, and we had little support and even less experience in the specifics of my mom's unique and complex co-occurring conditions.

The people with the knowledge and experience to help inform her care, and to identify problems that may arise before they get worse, were located miles away at the clinic. The nurses, physician assistants, and physicians who had seen hundreds of cases, had years of medical education, and access to additional information were not at home with us.

Our knowledge and skills were good. I can take a blood pressure accurately in the back of a moving ambulance, I can look up side effects, and I can read clinical literature. We were well prepared, but were nevertheless still flying blind at home.

The only time we were able to access the knowledge and skills located at the clinic was when we were physically at the clinic, or when something was so unclear that we had to call. We were fortunate because I was well aware of what I did not know and when it was time to seek additional counsel.

For many people, knowing when to call for help or even identifying important warning signs is impossible. Thus, patients and their caregivers are largely left with static lists and recommendations from their providers despite changing patient conditions. Patients, when discharged, may have very different needs three weeks later.

We took important steps to provide the best care for my mom, who, even under the ideal circumstances, was in a precarious situation and did not need any mistakes.

It came down to collecting data in our pink binder. We recorded symptoms, tracked medication administration, tracked meals, tracked how she was feeling, and tracked her activity levels at home. We wanted to provide the medical professionals with the most information possible, to ensure they had the full picture to inform their decisions.

When we were at the clinic, we requested paper copies of all the lab results, took notes, and followed up on prescriptions and medical devices recommended for her. We tracked the progress and efficacy of medications and their common side effects. Fortunately, we had some knowledge, some resources, and the time to do this. We had a team of full-time caregivers. Many patients are not so lucky.

My mom's condition, up to this point, had changed on a weekly basis. Some weeks we saw marked improvement while others proved to be major disappointments as lab values came back and adjustments were needed. During the good weeks, we were able to reduce the frequency of clinic visits, which was an absolute relief for my mom (the journey to and from the clinic in Atlanta rush-hour traffic was long, tiresome, and painful). But this meant we were at home, once again caring for a patient with complex, multiple chronic conditions, administering too many medications, managing her diet, helping her with her activities of daily living, making her comfortable, and trying to take care of ourselves, too.

Patients' conditions change frequently while they self-manage care at home and more so if they are managing multiple chronic conditions. If these changes are relevant to physician and clinician decision-making, then more data collection activities can help to ensure good decision-making, proactive care management, and treatment plan compliance.

There must be a better way to do this than on paper in a pink binder.

* * *

Modern medicine is typically based on the analysis of patient diagnostic data like lab tests, blood tests, patient self-reported information, medical histories, and subsequent analysis by a physician with years of education and experience. Modern medicine has brought along additional data points like genetic testing, more easily accessible trend analysis in electronic health records, and more precise lab measurement tools and imaging technologies.

Needless to say, data is crucial regardless of type. You cannot diagnose, treat, and educate patients without *some* information off of which to work. For years, patient data was locked and essentially unusable in paper-based medical records.

Within the confines of medical decision-making, healthcare has done a pretty good job of improving data collection, the ability to quickly run lab tests, and take other physiological measurements. But the issue is just that "within the confines of medical decision-making." We know that a person's and population's health is a product of many factors besides the physiological lab tests, genetics, and other prioritized medical values that are only collected during physical visits.

Patients have difficulty navigating the system, matching with proper treatments, managing chronic conditions, overcoming barriers to successful treatments, affording medications, getting to appointments, receiving care that views them as more than a set of individual lab values, and overall receiving support from the system when they are outside of it.

These are the problems that need to be solved far more than a 10 percent improvement in specificity for a lab test, which is too often the focus of healthcare innovation discussions. That is where and why interest in information technology used to support healthcare payment and delivery is growing, as organizations and people in healthcare begin to accept and adopt the mindset that healthcare is more than just medicine and clinic visits.

Thus, collecting data is crucial. There are two areas of improvement in data collection that will be supported and enhanced by digital health technologies:

1. New data collection locations and frequencies
2. New data types

Under the current system of institution-based, episodic, and reactive healthcare services, the points of data collection are fully dependent on patients walking into a facility or engaging with healthcare professionals in person.

You go to an annual physical, you go to your quarterly endocrinology or cardiology appointments, and you fill out paper forms where you answer questions for your physician, they run blood tests, and they do physical exams where they record findings in your medical record that is likely now electronic.

These visits and the data generated from them are then stored in electronic health records, for retrieval by anyone who has permission and credentials to access your information. This is often only the physician and immediate staff. Too often, it is even difficult for patients to get access to their own records.

In healthcare, this is where all the data is collected for making decisions, monitoring conditions, and tracking progress. For some people, this means data is collected once a year. For people with decently managed chronic conditions, this means four to six times a year. For people with more intense services with complex conditions in poor maintenance, this may be more frequent like twice a month or more.

Once, twice, or six times a year is at most 1.6 percent of days in the year in which health data is collected by the health system. But visits only last about fifteen to twenty minutes. So, the time during a year in which data is collected is more like 120 minutes out of 525,600 minutes in a year, which is 0.02 percent of a person's year—despite the fact that conditions and health are experienced each day with fluctuations occurring frequently.

But thanks to recent innovations in mobile, wearable, and other information technologies, we can now do better. The popularization of smartphones, smartwatches, home-based Wi-Fi, 5G networks, Bluetooth, and other Internet of Things (IoT) technologies have enabled the acceleration of home and person-based technologies that can be leveraged for data collection in new locations and more frequently.

If we want to view health as a longitudinal experience with longitudinal effects and outcomes, then data collection more frequently along that time window is necessary to most accurately understand a person's health.

The ability to wear devices, answer questions, input data, and generally to collect more health-related data from smartphones, home-based computers, and wearables as people progress through their day-to-day lives is incredible.

Now, the health system can extend its data collection reach into people's daily lives, in order to monitor for the benefit of health. That data can, in turn, be used to generate actionable information, make predictions through analytics, and to store information for when it is needed.

* * *

Montuno's application, Dosecast, is a simple medication management app available on all smartphones. Again, this application allows people who take multiple daily medications, typically those with chronic illness, to receive reminders, to track their schedules, to records doses and symptoms, and to receive refill reminders.

This is a simple technology, but one that solves a big problem for patients. Instead of using paper calendars to remember medications, this allows for that capability on smartphones with a single click and access to the full record of medications taken in one's daily life.

Reminders and tracking capabilities help patients to self-manage their conditions, to prevent missed or accidental doses, and to help patients seamlessly integrate complex medication regimens into their daily lives.

The medication adherence, health status, and symptom data are then made available to physicians and care managers. Now, physicians can see that their patients are taking their medications as prescribed, that they are reporting good health, and have access to the full medication lists—even if they themselves did not prescribe the medication (because, for example, the patient also sees a cardiologist).

Perhaps, this patient was not scheduled for another visit for three months. But now, a quick glance at a dashboard by a physician can provide additional monitoring for patients. This type of solution allows for daily data to be collected on patients, wherever they might be outside the four walls of the healthcare organization.

These technologies also allow for new types of data to be collected. In Dosecast, a patient's daily medication adherence is tracked, which is impossible during a typical office visit. The patient is able to report symptoms and subjective health status on a scale of one to ten. The simple question of "how would you rate your health today?" is a powerful tool to understand the health of a patient. It provides a reliable and simple method for physicians to see how patients are feeling, without more complicated data collected in the patient's home.

A patient who has reported a 9/10 for the past two months but starts to report a 4/10 for a few days might need some extra support or might merit a phone call. A physician can then reach out and set up an office visit, phone call, or video chat to review medications and symptoms. Or, better yet, this process can be automated without the need for a physician to review. An appointment can be suggested to the patient and can then be remotely scheduled.

Surveys, medication adherence, home-based lab tests, activity levels, sleep schedules, blood sugar, electronic-cardio grams (ECG), heart rate, respiratory rate, blood pressure, self-reported health status, symptoms, diet, eating schedules, and falls are examples of the new types of data that can be collected easily, cheaply, and in a format that enables more aggressive data analysis and automation.

I wear an Apple Watch every day. All I have to do is put it on in the morning after it charges all night. From this, my heart rate, activity level, exercise, falls, and ECG can be collected and stored. As a healthy individual, my physician can take this information and suggest activities and behaviors to help me stay that way. For a patient who has a chronic illness, this information can inform the physician's recommendations for lifestyle changes backed by data or can inform care providers when an individual may be at risk for future deterioration.

"I see you haven't been very active over the past few months," says a physician to a patient with hypertension, at-risk for developing more dangerous cardiovascular conditions.

"I don't have time to exercise," says the patient.

"What if you committed to taking the stairs whenever possible?"

This type of new data taken from a patient's daily life provides the ability to identify and discuss lifestyle diagnoses and to track progress. Patients with atrial fibrillation—a cardiovascular condition experienced by a large number of people—can also provide new reports taken from their Apple Watch on a more frequent basis. If the physician notices a problem then a medication dose change, behavioral modification, or office visit for more follow-up can be suggested. Instead of waiting for the next appointment or for a heart attack to occur, the health system can be proactive with a low amount of effort through enhanced mobile data collection.

If a patient doesn't seem to be taking their medications based on mobile data collection, the physician and care manager have access to his information and that patient is flagged in the monitoring system for non-adherence. Upon a phone call, the care manager learns that the patient doesn't understand how to take the medication, and has been skipping doses to "stretch the medication" because it is too expensive to fill each month.

The patient is then referred to a social worker who helps the patient get assistance for medication co-pays, discovers that the patient has difficulty reading, and refers the patient to a patient educator who can help them learn how to self-manage the condition. Without mobile data collection, this process may not have been engaged for months until a scheduled office visit wherein the patient could have ended up in the hospital due to medication non-adherence, or the issue may not have been identified at all because it did not come up in conversation.

The previous two examples rely on a physician mediating and decision making, which is important. But this type of data collection also lends itself to more sophisticated analysis and process automation. The ability to use this new data in combination with claims and electronic health record data is now possible as well. The more data available, the more predictions can be made using the data, and thus the more processes can be automated to support the patient.

Instead of paper in a pink binder, we could have been provided an electronic means by which to track at-home care and enter data. If there was a problem, nurses and physicians back in the clinic could have been alerted and supportive processes could have been initiated proactively.

For patients who are less prepared and knowledgeable, this type of support is crucial to the future of healthcare service delivery. Even for us, the knowledge and experience available at the clinic were necessary to ensure care was being provided properly and safely.

Building technologies that collect new data in new locations and more frequently is necessary to build a health system that is proactive and views patient experiences as long-term, rather than episodic and cross-sectional snapshots.

# CHAPTER 20

# TECHNOLOGY THAT STORES AND EXCHANGES

———

"When are you going back to school?"

My mom asked this abruptly, one day after we got back from a long day at the clinic. After we got her settled at home—and after my taking a week off school for the second time in the semester—she asked me to go back to school; it was clear that I had planned on staying home. Knowing that my life goals and plans could be derailed even slightly due to her condition was too much for my mom, who had worked tirelessly to help me get to Georgetown. So, I returned to finish the last few weeks of the semester, and the time I took off was fairly unimpactful thanks to supportive professors.

"The inpatient facility and the outpatient clinic were on separate EHRs," I said to my information systems professor upon my return.

"Really?"

"Yes, and they use duplicate records with a paper chart and an Epic EHR on the inpatient floor," I said. We were both shocked by the visceral truth of what we theoretically discussed weekly in class and knew to be a daily struggle in healthcare.

It was not long until I returned home for the summer after finishing the semester. While my mom was still at home and had not been readmitted, things were not going as well as I had been led to believe.

My mom was losing weight, and her ability to move on her own was declining rather than improving as I had hoped. She started to experience vision issues due to an eye infection during her time in the hospital. And her ability to move fluid from her lungs was still poor, as her heart was still recovering from damage that likely occurred from the chemotherapy.

Her congestive heart failure, leukemia, blood fungal infection, and eye infection were all still present and making her extremely uncomfortable, not to mention contributing heavily to the challenges of managing her care.

These new developments required ongoing appointments with four new physician specialists. This included an eye surgeon at Emory University Hospital, a gastroenterologist, an infectious disease specialist, and a cardiologist in addition to her hematology-oncology clinic appointments. Each, of course, with their own EHR system, no communication with each other, and their own prescription pads.

\* \* \*

Unite Us provides an excellent example of the application of technology to a major movement in healthcare.

If patients have multiple co-occurring conditions and risk factors then our single-minded organizations fail to provide comprehensive and effective medical care. Specialization is great for developing depth of knowledge and effectiveness at treating specific issues, but in a complex system like that of the human body and human experience, medical service organizations around specialties is not the best way to provide effective care.

So then, how can we ensure adequate depth of expertise while providing more comprehensive and coordinated services to patients?

Once again, it comes down to coordination and information. In this case, after the information is collected, it must be stored and shared effectively to enable collaboration and fully-informed decision making.

Whether shared in-person or shared electronically, the ability to provide more comprehensive care to patients requires good information and communication between the specialized experts.

In some cases, organizations like The Cleveland Clinic, one of the world's top hospital systems, have pioneered "team-based care" that puts a patient's various specialists on a team to work together when it comes to decision making and developing diagnoses and treatments.

Unfortunately for those of us who live in areas too far to take advantage of the Cleveland Clinic, we are stuck with the same fragmented and disconnected system to provide care. The Cleveland Clinic is one of the best-funded healthcare organizations, and is thus able to do things that many facilities and systems are unable to accomplish.

However, this is an area where technology is able to provide a major benefit when it comes to coordinating and delivering more comprehensive care to patients with chronic illness. Technology, digitized clinical data, and the need to do so create the perfect environment for this type of innovation to drive major change.

\* \* \*

We were seeing five different physicians who operate five different practices, and, therefore, five separate medical record systems. Our now-not-so-little pink binder made the trip with us between various delivery organizations and appointments, to ensure that we were able to track and communicate information to different healthcare professionals in order to make an attempt at ensuring comprehensive care.

Besides the separate organizations with separate data systems, the hematology-oncology clinic where we spent most of our time, and the one that staffs the inpatient bone marrow transplant unit, is on a separate electronic health record system than the outpatient clinic where we would travel to frequently after my mom's initial hospitalization.

The critical information collected and recorded on my mom's inpatient treatment journey was not readily available for use once we were sent home, and vice versa. Providers would have to make phone calls and send emails to ask questions. This is a terribly inefficient system, and one that does not prioritize the patient and the need for complete information on a patient's conditions.

Each physician only knew what we were able to tell them with regard to my mom's other four physicians, making our own ability to collect, store, and exchange data through a pink binder the best method available to us during this process.

Our first visit to the Emory Eye Institute was an hour-and-fifteen-minute drive from our house, after a lengthy day at the hematology-oncology clinic the day before. We arrived and sat in the waiting room for thirty minutes before being moved to another waiting room in the back of the clinic, but still one step closer to the subsequent twenty-minute wait in the exam room.

As the physician entered the room, he introduced himself and moved to begin examining my mom's eye.

"Can you please wash your hands before the exam," requested one of our family members.

"Oh, yes, sure," said the physician.

"She's a leukemia patient, so we have to be careful about that."

Prior to the first visit, this physician had no idea my mom was a very recent leukemia patient. The records sent to him from the previous ophthalmology consultation a few weeks before were relevant only to the eye condition and reason for referral.

After seeing many patients that day, it was very possible that he came into contact with some pathogen with the ability to harm a very sick and immunocompromised patient. Without our vigilance and willingness to speak up, a dangerous situation may have occurred.

While his job was to examine, diagnose, and treat an eye infection that was impacting my mom's vision, her other conditions were still present and impacting her overall health.

* * *

As mobile, wearable, and existing data collection methods accelerate and become more efficient at collecting new types of data at new locations and more frequently, there comes a growing need to ensure that the interoperability failures of electronic health records do not get repeated again—meaning that information *must* be shared and utilized effectively between and within organizations.

Data collected is only useful in healthcare if it is turned into actionable information and it is available at the right time, in the right form, and for the right people. Thus, innovations that allow for the effective storage and exchange of data will become necessary for delivering more effective care.

Delivery organizations entering into more risk-based contracts and accountable care-like payment models will need to ensure that their information systems and digital health technologies are able to support the care needed by patients, in order to successfully meet the obligations under the new incentives.

## CHAPTER 21

# TECHNOLOGY THAT PREDICTS

―――

"I wish we could have known that she was at risk for that heart complication," I said to my grandma as we were sitting in the waiting room of the cardiologist's office during a routine evaluation. "This is a bad complication when she is still fighting cancer. I can't help but wonder if we could have known that this would happen and used different medications."

As I thought back to the middle of my mom's inpatient stay—I was in Delaware visiting my grandfather for the weekend. It was a short train ride up to Delaware from Washington DC, and he and I both continued to struggle with my mom's condition as she stayed confined in the Atlanta hospital.

After he picked me up from the train, we stopped for a short dinner at a local seafood restaurant, then drove back to my grandparents' house. Soon after returning home, I received a call from my dad.

As soon as I answered the phone, I could tell something was wrong.

"Son, your mom's being moved to the ICU because of her heart, and we think it's a good idea for everyone to come back home," my dad said with an attempt to say those words without fear, but with a terror we could both feel.

"Okay, we will get on a flight tomorrow morning," I said as the reality of the situation produced the sinking feeling that I had experiences several times by that point. My grandpa, who recognized my change in demeanor at the beginning of the call, sat down in the chair across the room with an expressionless face and an equal share of understanding, even without knowing what had been said.

We booked a flight, flew to Atlanta, and went straight to the hospital. As I approached the ICU, I knew the outlook and it was not good. Most patients do not leave the ICU.

At this point, she had been fully reliant on modern medicine and biotechnology to keep her alive for a few days on both the bone marrow transplant floor and during this week-long stint in the intensive care unit (ICU), due to a rapid deterioration in her heart's ability to pump blood that likely resulted from the chemotherapy.

I will never forget my conversation with her as we sat in the room alone together. My mom was already a small person at 5'2" inches tall, but now looked even smaller. She was a mess of tubes and monitors, disappearing into the large white ICU bed.

She had gone from a marathon-running fifth-grade teacher with enough energy to manage a classroom full of thirty kids to being unable to rise from the bed, fed through a tube, and in a precarious life or death situation. I took the opportunity to have what I expected to be one of the last conversations I would ever have with my mom.

As I sat in tears, she mustered all she could to maintain the conversation with me, also knowing and accepting her proximity to death. I sat, like a good student learning from his favorite teacher, and took notes.

As I walked out of that ICU when visitor hours ended, later that day, I could not help but wonder if something could have changed the course of her disease and subsequent treatment-related outcomes up to this point. If only we could have known that the combination of drugs, her unique profile, and other events would have led us to this point, perhaps we could have prevented any number of events leading up to this point.

This was an important moment for my understanding of patient care in our current system. What if we could do something differently?

* * *

"My parents got divorced when I was ten, so I moved in with my grandfather, who was like my dad," said Jerry Wilmink as he started to tell me about his career journey. Like many innovators and entrepreneurs I interviewed, Jerry immediately began his professional story with his childhood. For people who dedicate their lives to the risky, unstable, and uncertain business of innovative start-up companies, there is often a higher purpose driving their actions.

"My grandfather, who was in his mid-seventies, suffered from Lewy Body Dementia which is somewhere in between Alzheimer's and Dementia," explained Jerry.

From an early age, Jerry was exposed to the challenges of chronic illness. As he grew up, he would attend Vanderbilt University, in Nashville, T.N., where he studied Biomedical Engineering in undergrad and, eventually, through the completion of a doctoral program.

Now, as Jerry Wilmink, PhD., he would go on to set up a new spectroscopy lab for the Department of Defense, and come to manage the Air Force Small Business Innovation Research (SBIR) grant program—a program often leveraged by start-ups to gain initial R&D funding. Part innovation accelerator, part venture-capital organization, the SBIR program is a major federal initiative to promote innovation and research across the different federal agencies, including the National Institutes of Health.

During his time at the DoD, Jerry would come to learn how much he enjoyed building things from scratch, would go on to publish scientific papers, begin an executive MBA program, and come to understand the level to which bureaucracy and slow-moving innovation brings him down. The combination between his professional experiences during this time and a later personal life event would inspire Jerry to leave his stable, tenured track position to pursue solutions that truly solve tangible problems.

"My grandfather, again suffering from his dementia, fell en route from his bedroom to the bathroom. He laid there for hours until my grandma found him. He ended up living through that event, but passed away not too long after in 2010."

Jerry credits this episode and subsequent loss of the man that raised him as the catalyst for wanting to take action.

\* \* \*

Technology is becoming more and more ubiquitous in our society. As mobile technology continues to accelerate in capabilities, speed, and adoption, the possibility for innovation that leverages these devices is tremendous. The ability to solve real problems using these technologies is incredible.

Healthcare is full of data sets that already exist and are unused or underused by organizations. Developing solutions and products that leverage these existing sets of data will continue to dominate the world of digital health technology. But as mobile products and technologies continue to dominate the consumer landscape, the ability to collect never-before-available data now exists.

But data collected for the sake of collecting data is not particularly useful. In order to help transform the delivery of care to a more proactive orientation, something needs to be done with that data to transform it into information, knowledge, and to make it actionable.

When it comes to a proactive healthcare delivery system, that means making predictions and assigning risk to patients for a certain outcome in order to intervene before things get out of control. Just like risk factors for chronic illness—like diet, exercise, and social factors—new and currently available data can be used to understand new risk factors for certain specific events like falling, readmission to the hospital, and medication non-adherence.

Prediction, once data exists, leverages that data to produce actionable information the health system can use to intervene in a patient's condition before they end up in the emergency department, inpatient care, or requiring intensive specialist services.

\* \* \*

For people like Jerry, motivated by personal life experience, the natural place to look is to the patient. Leveraging his engineering experience and expertise, Jerry set out to solve a problem he witnessed firsthand at the patient-level. He looked at solutions that already existed on the market, and discovered that most fall-related senior technologies helped people call for help and to receive help quicker once they have already fallen.

"Reacting quicker to an airplane that crashed is not as important as predicting that a crash will happen," quipped Jerry.

Jerry looked at the existing technologies and decided that it would be ideal if the technologies could pick up behaviors that precluded a fall. Rather than simply facilitating a response to a fall, Jerry wanted to have wearable technologies that can alert to the potential for a fall to happen based on a person's behavior. He wanted to predict the fall outcome *before* it happens.

Thus, Jerry founded Wisewear, a company that develops biosensing wearable that can predict falls and other health outcomes. Jerry raised eight million in venture funding to develop the technologies, and enlisted technology experts and fashion designers to bring his vision to life.

"We had a hearing aid that could detect balance and collect data, but we needed to raise more money to bring it to market after it was developed," he said.

That is when Jerry was introduced to Satish Movva, the CEO and founder of CarePredict. Satish was motivated by a similar story to Jerry's.

Satish developed the first electronic medical record for the Palm Pilot and original SaaS platforms for the Home Care and Home Health industries before starting CarePredict after caring for his mother and father at home. After a few emergency department visits, Satish also realized there was little technology existing in the space. As a technology guy himself, he set out to do something about it.

After looking at products on the market, like ambient motion sensors that could be placed on refrigerators or on beds to monitor activity, Satish realized that there were two key problems. One, these sensors did not produce patient-specific data that could be linked to any one individual. And two, these sensors were unable to determine if the motion was created by Mom and Dad going about their lives in a healthy, happy manner or was simply the dog walking around.

"He knew that wasn't enough," said Jerry as he drew the parallels to his own story with WiseWear.

In order to help solve the problems associated with older adults living at home on their own, both Jerry and Satish knew that new devices were necessary.

Satish founded CarePredict in 2013, the first to market with a solution that detects changes in daily activities and predicts potential issues like falls, urinary tract infections (UTIs), depression, and malnutrition. In 2018, CarePredict purchased WiseWear, Jerry's disruptor in the senior care space.

Thus, the product produced by CarePredict has been on the market for several years now in both the US and Japan. And it works well.

The product is a wearable device, worn by an individual to understand and analyze their activities of daily living. The system collects motion and other bio-sensed data from the wearer, and compiles it into a profile that establishes a baseline of normal activity.

Thus, data profiles for the individual and their normal healthy behavior can be tracked as they wear the device in their daily lives. This is when the power of the tool becomes clear.

Items like the individual's personalized drinking gesture, personalized eating gesture, how they wash their face, the room they are in, and how they bathe are all measured and a baseline of "normal" is established. Now that the baseline for activities is established, the ability to predict or identify risk for certain outcomes is possible.

"We can predict and identify individuals that are at risk for and experiencing depression. If we see a decrease in baseline activity levels, reductions in social time where the individual is spending time alone instead of in the community, and eating durations decreased from the longitudinal baseline; we identify that individual," says Jerry.

Falls are the obvious low-hanging fruit, and the CarePredict platform performs well in that area as well. But the ability to identify more conditions—like depression—which has physical risk factors and motion-based hallmarks, is also incredible.

This type of prediction using mobile collected data to solve costly problems exists for numerous applications on the market already, and new start-ups pop up each day looking to make their mark on a new application for this type of solution.

* * *

CarePredict is already seeing fast adoption in the home care space. It has been adopted by the largest provider of home care services in Japan and has raised $18 million in venture funding. The company is doing well, and their technology has undoubtedly saved patients and families from the suffering associated with falls and subsequent emergency department experiences.

CarePredict was piloted in senior living facilities to enable the program to learn and have the support of staff during the study period. According to Jerry, who is looking to publish the results in a peer-reviewed journal, the solution has reduced hospitalizations by 27 percent, increased staff response time 27-41 percent, decreased monthly fall rates by 37 percent, and the average length of stay for the individual in the assisted living facility, rather than deterioration to a skilled nursing facility, increased.

These metrics tell the wider health system an important story.

These types of solutions, when built to solve patient problems, can have a major impact. Reducing hospitalizations cuts costs by tens of thousands of dollars, decreasing falls prevents suffering and subsequent health issues associated with them, and quality of life is improved by allowing individuals to remain in assisted living—rather than in a hospital bed.

Jerry and Satish set out to solve a patient's problem they had each witnessed first-hand. Leveraging mobile technology to collect new data, analyzing that data in real-time, and empowering existing healthcare organizations to use the new information to improve patient care has, in turn, produced significant benefits.

"CarePredict collects the most accurate data on activity and behavior and changes to these, we know, are precursors before a health decline," says Jerry.

Changes to activities and motion of individuals collected by these wearables are the risk factors for the targeted outcome, like a fall or depression. When these risk factors are identified in an individual in real-time, that individual is flagged in the system and family members, care teams, or assisted living facilities are notified accordingly.

The other benefit of CarePredict's program is that it collects data *passively*. The best technologies add value, solve problems, and often do so through passive work. The patient simply has to wear the device and it works after an initial setup period. There is not significant user-input. This makes this device relatively accessible and useable by anyone who can wear it.

The passively collected data is then stored and available to be used for the prediction of any target outcome that may have risk factors, indicated by the type of motion data collected by the wearable. Depression and fall risk are, as stated, two factors identified specifically by Jerry, but other conditions based on motion and behavior changes that preclude their development can also be added to prediction algorithms.

Data in healthcare—like that collected by CarePredict, or the vast amounts of claims and clinical data collected by the healthcare system already—is useless unless it is analyzed and presented in the form of actionable information.

"You cannot just do a data dump on the staff. Taking the data, making the predictions, and identifying the high-risk individuals is necessary," says Jerry.

*  *  *

Prediction is crucial. Understanding risk factors that can be identified and linked to a specific patient is necessary to intervene, before that patient experiences the target outcome or ends up in the emergency department, inpatient hospital, or requiring more intensive services.

While CarePredict set out to collect data that was previously unavailable in the system, other companies are leveraging existing data sets to transform data into actionable information for healthcare payment and delivery organizations.

Companies like i2i Population Health, UnitedHealth Group's Optum, and other companies perform predictive analytics on the existing claims and EHR data collected in vast quantities in the health system to identify risky patients, target interventions, and to assist in the transition to value-based care such as that under the ACO model.

While not necessarily performed in real-time as is necessary to be truly proactive, these examples of predictive analytics using existing data are also driving change and benefit to the patient. Health plans can identify members at risk for future hospitalization and can notify primary care physicians, alert the patient, or reach out directly through telehealth services and nurses that staff care management departments.

Hospitals with predictive risk engines operating on their clinical data located in their electronic health records can better understand the risk of readmissions at the point of discharge. For low-risk patients, they can limit their services.

For high-risk patients, they can tailor more intensive services aimed at reducing that risk. Sending someone home with nurse visits, admitting them to a skilled nursing facility for more rehabilitation, and remotely monitoring their progress using in-home monitors to collect data is becoming the norm. All powered by prediction.

Even within hospitals, just as my mom received treatment for weeks with many decisions made, there are new technologies that leverage the vast amounts of clinical data to make predictions and to better match the patient with a diagnosis or treatment by leveraging large amounts of data. This is called clinical decision support, and it relies on similar technologies plus analytic methods to help physicians predict risk and select the best options for a particular patient.

These companies sell their suites of solutions to ACOs, hospital systems, and health insurance companies looking to reduce the cost of their patient populations in a similar manner to CarePredict, just leveraging existing data that is often under- or un-utilized for these purposes.

So, from this, it is possible to learn a few important aspects about the use of digital health technologies that predict in the healthcare space:

1. Data is either sourced from existing sources, or can be collected using new methods such as mobile wearables and mobile devices.
2. Longitudinal data (data collected over time) is the basis upon which predictions are made and improved.

3. The more data points the better, i.e., passively collecting data on wearables can be continuous.
4. Prediction has the ability to enhance the delivery system so as to identify at-risk patients, which enables the system to intervene when necessary.
5. Prediction and the use of data can, overall, help identify patients at risk for a certain outcome, and can subsequently match those patients with appropriate treatments and interventions.

\* \* \*

In light of recent activity in payment reform that has led to a new focus on cost and the actual health of individuals receiving care from the healthcare delivery system, solutions like those provided by CarePredict and other predictive analytics companies are the future of care delivery.

Prior to the adoption of alternative payment models, value-based payments, the ACO model, and other models that place the delivery organizations at risk for cost (and therefore patient outcomes), these types of technologies would be adopted slowly and by organizations that happen to be innovative by nature.

To drive more impactful and widespread change, these types of technologies are growing in concert with payment reform models that have been gaining awareness and adoption throughout the health system. Payment reform critics say that the system has very little ability to manage patient care outside the four walls of facilities, and can "only do so much."

That was true until technology reached the point at which data collection and subsequent analysis have become health game-changers. The health system is now sitting in the perfect storm to allow for patient-level improvements in care, driven by digital health technologies that can now be adopted due to major incentive changes and payment reform efforts.

# CHAPTER 22

# CARING FOR THE REMOTE PATIENT

———

Things were going pretty well at home. It was now June and we had come a long way since mid-February, when my mom was rushed to the emergency department, and, certainly, since mid-April, when she was released from the hospital to our home. We had overcome the challenges during the inpatient stay, ICU stint, in the transition between inpatient and outpatient care, and we were learning how to make sure everything went smoothly. We as caregivers, and my mom as a patient, were learning how to navigate and best manage her conditions.

For a period, we were in a pretty solid "groove" and in high spirits fueled by small, gradual improvements to my mom's condition. Our confidence in managing her treatments at home was improving after we learned some lessons through some serious work.

We were living at our home in Atlanta, which had been transformed into a home-based hospital with assistive devices, tinted windows, and plenty of medical supplies arriving on almost a daily basis.

"Hi, can I speak to the on-call nurse?" I would say as I called to ask an occasional question, or to ask for recommendations to administer an "as needed" or "PRN" medication. Most often this medication was Lasix, a diuretic, that is used to help the body remove excess fluid by inducing the kidneys to remove more water. My mom's heart was not pumping enough volume, so there would be fluid built up around the heart, a condition known as congestive heart failure. This issue began prior to discharge from the hospital and was the primary reason for her stint in the ICU.

We would use Lasix to remove that fluid when it built up. I would listen to her lungs for crackles that indicate fluid with my EMT stethoscope, and I would call to discuss the condition with a nurse who usually suggested that I administer Lasix. The management of fluid around the heart and lungs is crucial to keep congestive heart failure (CHF) patients oxygenated and able to breathe sufficiently. CHF is one of the major cost-driving chronic illnesses in the US. It is a common co-morbidity for patients with hypertension, obesity, diabetes, hyperlipidemia, and metabolic syndrome.[31] In fact, in Medicare, 55 percent of patients with congestive heart failure have five or more additional conditions.[32]

---

31  *American Heart Association*

32  *Centers for Medicare and Medicaid Services. "Chronic conditions among Medicare beneficiaries, chartbook, 2012 edition." Baltimore, MD 11 (2012): 15-21*

We used that pink three-ring binder with elementary school-esque colorful plastic dividers to keep track of all her test results, documents, and to record the medication administered on a daily basis. We recorded her vital signs like blood pressure, heart rate, respiratory rate, blood glucose, medication adherence, and her eating schedule as she was still receiving food through a PEG tube to maintain nutrition (her appetite had been fully absent since chemotherapy).

Keeping that data and the records all in one place was crucial to ensuring different physicians understood her care and had all the information possible to make good decisions. It was our bible, our management software, our electronic health record, and the thing that allowed us to keep track of all the things we needed to in order to manage her care at home.

During this time, our only interaction with the health system was during the few weekly clinic visits that varied, and the occasional call I would make to ask a medication question. We received very little support from the healthcare system. They provided us with knowledge and treatments, but it was on us to monitor her condition and manage it at home.

We set up many of our processes and the ways in which we cared for my mom based on recommendations from my cousin Bridget and my great-aunt Viv, who both work in the healthcare industry. Bridget, an ICU nurse, and Aunt Viv, who works in the home care space, were both helpful in identifying products, setting up our pink binder, and transitioning my mom into the home environment from the hospital.

I had received my national emergency medical technician (EMT) certification just a month before my mom was rushed to the emergency department, so I was well-trained in taking vital signs, moving patients, and understanding important aspects of patient care and risks associated with medications. In addition to my formal education in navigating the health system, this clinical experience served us well in helping to both transport and provide care to my mom.

Despite the help and the support of our qualified family, I cannot stress enough the difficulty we experienced and how challenging the home-based management of my mom's care truly was during those long, hot months in Georgia where days at home caring for my mom were long and hard. I think it is fair to say that we were as prepared and qualified as we could have been.

It was at this point that I questioned the system once again. What about those patients and families who do not have such a deep bench of expertise, help, and experience? Most patients and families, after all, don't. We were fortunate and despite our access to information and the ability to understand it well, it was a struggle.

For most people, and those without these skills and access to information, how can the health system step into the home to better manage and support patients who need help and monitoring? Patients spend the majority of their time outside the walls of the healthcare delivery organization, but still, the system has failed to build itself in a way that recognizes and supports this crucial part of a patient's health journey.

A system built to support the patient in moving toward better health, or maintaining current chronic illness would recognize that the behaviors and challenges with healthcare in the home have a major impact on the success of treatments and any potential errors.

But this is changing, thanks to technology. Prior to risk-based contracting and alternative payment models, there was no incentive for the system to invest in home-based technologies because office visits and inpatient stays were financially incentivized.

The system has quite a way to go in supporting the patient in the home and in their daily lives, but advances in mobile technology and new incentives are paving the way for a better future.

* * *

Many of the technologies introduced already like CarePredict, Dosecast, PillPack, and others are all unified along one theme: bringing care delivery and condition management support to the home or community, to meet the patient where they may be located more frequently than in a medical facility.

What happens when patients are sent home outside the four walls of the health system's institutions? How can we predict negative outcomes? How can we get patients out of the hospital and back into their homes successfully? How can we ensure that they stay there and get better? How can we prevent readmissions once a patient is home? How can we better connect the patient to the knowledge and skills of healthcare professionals to ensure adequate care for the times they are on their own?

The home is where patients spend a great deal of time. When patients are discharged from the hospital, they often go home or to a rehabilitation facility. When patients receive a new chronic illness diagnosis, they return home. When patients can live their daily lives with chronic illnesses, they return home. The home is where medications are stored. The home is where caregivers help patients navigate their care. The home is where people charge and store their mobile devices. The home is where people prepare meals and choose to sit on the couch all day or not. The home, in short, is where health and wellness *live*.

Mobile-based, wearable, and voice technologies offer the ability to collect and analyze data into actionable information to inform the health system's ability to intervene in the home or wherever that patient may be. Too often, people see technology innovation in healthcare as a means to automate existing processes. In many cases, that can and will happen to drive efficient administrative processes that limit activities that can affect patient condition improvements like education, research, and analysis of patient data. But in other cases, it makes more sense to extend and enhance the reach of medical professionals to build a synergistic relationship between the technologies and the people-based operations.

The home is where the health system needs to be, to be able to predict a potential hospitalization and to keep patients in the home. It is impossible to have physicians and nurses in every home as needed to ensure adequate care and management of conditions. It is also impossible to expect that most people can fully understand and adequately manage their own care all the time. Likewise, it is near impossible to teach a machine to make recommendations in the way a human mind can analyze variables. A complementary approach is necessary. Technology has the ability to collect data, analyze data, sort patients based on risk, automate administrative tasks, and visualize data in a user-friendly way to promote efficiency and facilitate communication. These capabilities extend reach, complement existing human capabilities, and allow for the creation of new models of care.

Mobile and wearable technologies have unlimited potential to collect data and to connect the health system to the patient like never before. This process is all about bringing the right knowledge and capabilities of medicine to the right patients, more frequently, at the right times, and in the right ways.

Patients and caregivers are limited in their ability to manage care at home and to identify warning signs, risk factors, and to generally ensure patients are optimizing their activities to ensure adequate maintenance of their health condition. Thus, it is necessary for any health system to extend its reach and capabilities into the home if health services are to improve health and wellness on a more consistent and effective basis.

∗ ∗ ∗

There are new approaches to solving this problem that have been dreamed up by innovative digital health entrepreneurs, major companies, and academics. Understanding the range of solutions helps to illustrate that there are many ways being explored to solve the fundamental divide between a patient's experience of care and the system's provision of it. Unifying them all is the principle of building new models that solve important problems and break down barriers to patients, while supporting them with data collection and analysis on a more frequent basis.

The following sections illustrate some of the major categories of innovations:

### PHYSICIAN VIDEO VISITS/TELEHEALTH

Companies like Teladoc and American Well allow patients to connect with a physician via video chat. Instead of requiring a patient to travel to a physician's office or other healthcare service delivery organization, patients can use their mobile device or computer to video conference with a physician in a similar manner to a regular office visit.

These technologies have been around for about a decade. They are tremendously helpful in bringing medical expertise to the patient's home, and in increasing access for rural individuals without geographic proximity to a physician.

For patients requiring significant effort to move, for those who work several jobs to support their families, and for anyone with a busy schedule, these technologies can provide convenient access to medical knowledge and advice toward maintaining good health.

As mobile and Internet of Things (IoT) data collection and diagnostic devices make their way into the home, our ability to increase the clinical effectiveness of telehealth video calls that mimic traditional office visits will accelerate.

The more data and analytic technologies that can be provided to physicians to better diagnose, tailor treatments, and identify barriers, the better the potential outcomes.

In fact, in a 2018 study by Deloitte on virtual healthcare, the top three benefits according to physicians are improved access to care (66 percent), improved patient satisfaction with care (52 percent), and staying connected with patients and caregivers in the home (45 percent).[33]

These three concepts clearly illustrate the traditional health system's first steps into the potential benefits that mobile, telehealth services can actually provide—it can provide a whole new proactive model of healthcare services. That last benefit—"staying connected with patients and caregivers"—touches on the core concept of this book: a model of care that is supportive and proactive, instead of reactive.

A health system built for the patient and one that prioritizes patient health and wellness requires more touchpoints and support for patients managing chronic conditions at home. Physicians are just now starting to recognize the level of contact and support that can be possible with modern digital technologies.

That all-too-common physician quote, "I can't control what happens when the patient leaves my office," is starting to

---

33   Deloitte 2018 Survey of US Physicians

become obsolete thanks to innovations that allow for more consistent and reliable contact between patient and physician.

Physicians have tremendous power to change behavior and to convince patients to follow recommendations based on their socio-economic backgrounds. Now, with more touch-points and supportive technologies, physicians can provide their medical knowledge to patients in a more proactive manner.

### PHYSIOLOGICAL AND WELLBEING REMOTE PATIENT MONITORING (RPM TECHNOLOGIES)

Now that video conferencing technology has become ubiquitous in our society, it is not unreasonable to conceive of video chatting with a physician in the comfort of one's home.

Companies like Montuno Software with Dosecast, CarePredict, and Vivify Health are all operating in a space that prioritizes mobile patient data collection to allow care providers and healthcare organizations to understand what happens when patients are not in their facilities. This allows for real-time adjustments and monitoring of patients using a variety of data.

At Montuno, we collect real-time medication lists, medication adherence, and health status data to help inform providers and family members about a patient's self-management. This platform allows for medication and treatment plan adherence, as well as patient self-reported health status to be shared with physicians in real-time to support patients in a data-driven manner.

CarePredict uses a custom-designed and built wearable to learn a patient's unique movements in order to predict various risks for medical conditions like depression or falls.

Vivify Health allows health systems and providers to collect various physiological data on patients remotely. Blood glucose, blood pressure, surveys, and other data using home devices are collected, analyzed, and presented to providers in real-time.

Vivify also links its data with existing electronic health records to allow for a seamless IT infrastructure, and then analyzes the data to allow for automated risk stratification. Now lab, health status, and patient health behaviors can be monitored at all times to predict and support patients in the home.

Companies like Vivify Health and others that collect information in the home for use by the health system fall under the category of "remote patient monitoring" (RPM). This term is used by the Centers for Medicare and Medicaid Services to label the reimbursement codes for this category. A recent advancement in payment, these codes incentivize delivery organizations and providers of care to begin performing these types of services.

This is another example of how payment incentives can shape the innovation and technology environment in the healthcare system. Vivify Health was born out of this reimbursement environment. These reimbursement codes are essentially an FFS payment-based incentive to get providers into using these types of data collection technologies to start bringing more comprehensive care into homes. While still FFS, this is a step in the right direction toward encouraging the adoption of technologies that can enhance the capabilities of medical professions and the delivery system.

These technologies are also being adopted by ACOs and ACO-like organizations due to the promise of better care, lower costs, and improved quality metrics. ACOs have to adopt these types of technologies in order to generate shared savings and reductions in emergency department, inpatient, and hospital readmissions for which they are responsible. Vivify Health touts large drops in hospital readmission rates (between 13 percent and 70 percent), lower emergency department visits (60 percent reduction), and lower inpatient hospitalizations (70 percent reduction) for large well-known healthcare delivery organizations like UPMC, Trinity Health, Ascension Health, and the Ontario Telemedicine Network.[34]

Patients using Vivify Health report high satisfaction as reported from a study with the University of Pittsburg Medical Center (UPMC), arguably one of the country's top health systems in terms of innovation.[35] Congestive heart failure (CHF) patients, like my mom, receiving care at UPMC were provided Vivify tablets and educational materials once they were discharged from the hospital.

UPMC employs a Kaiser Permanente (KP)-like model where they act as both health insurer and delivery organization leading to an interest in improving care, wellbeing, and

---

34  Vivify Health Case Studies
35  *Vivify Health: UPMC and Vivify – Improving Care Through Remote Patient Monitoring*

reducing costly points of service for members. This model, employed by KP and UPMC, is akin to the ACO because of similar incentives in place. Keeping patients healthier equals lower costs and higher profit margins.

Vivify and UPMC report the following outcomes:

*"Results have been promising among patients using Vivify. UPMC Health Plan members 65 and older who enroll in the program are now 74 percent less likely to be readmitted to the hospital within 90 days of discharge, and Medicare patients enrolled in the program were even higher, at 76 percent. The Vivify software has triaged more than 73,000 clinical information data points, helping nurses respond in priority to the 2 percent of data points showing clinical relevance in need of intervention. In this manner, Vivify has helped reduce the cost of care and reduce avoidable patient readmissions. Program compliance rates have also increased to 92 percent. This is especially important as strong compliance with the program gives clinicians the information they need to quickly intervene and help prevent unnecessary hospitalizations. It also gives UPMC confidence discharging patients from the hospital sooner without compromising outcomes."* [36]

These types of solutions have yet to gain widespread adoption, but the trend of mixing technology with home-based care services will continue to accelerate as market leaders—like Vivify—continue to prove results that help organizations focused on cost and care quality to achieve goals. Regardless of company or approach, the trend of these RPM solutions

---

36  *Ibid.*

will continue to gain traction either in the FFS reimbursement model, or under important new payment models that change incentives and thus require solutions like RPM to meet the shared savings goals of the program.

Adoption has been met with skepticism in the market. But with any technology, there is an adoption curve. It takes time for awareness and acceptance of new technologies due to organizational inertia that exists in any industry or society. It is tough to think outside the box that is our current system.

But for innovative organizations interested in performing at a higher level, these technologies are popping up in programs across the country. The end result is a more proactive health system that is beginning to address the barriers and challenges faced by patients in their pursuit of better health.

### BEHAVIOR CHANGE + LIFESTYLE "NUDGE APPS"

Many companies are looking to help support patients in a manner that is semi-independent of clinical health services through behavioral change. This area seeks to alter patient behavior in order to encourage and incentivize healthier activities, lifestyles, habits, and choices.

At Montuno, the Dosecast mobile application is an example of a habit-based behavioral intervention that helps individuals remember to take their medication. Using push notifications for reminders, dings from iPhones, and haptics (taps and touches) from wearables like the Apple Watch, Dosecast looks to help people with complex daily medication regimens stay on track. This helps encourage the positive health behavior of treatment plan adherence.

Other companies are taking approaches to alter other behavior using technologies, apps, digital checklists, push notifications, gamification, and other behavioral science-based techniques to change the way an individual acts so as to improve their health. This could be helping people choose a healthy meal tailored to their condition, providing incentives to exercise, helping patients with diabetes select meal ingredients that have a low impact on blood glucose, and the use of game-like applications to help encourage patient engagement (no-one likes to use a boring application).

Gamification and financial incentives, in particular, are two approaches that have gained popularity in the behavior change space. Gamification is essentially making a task more fun by adding points and small rewards to encourage engagement. You may have seen a program like this introduced by your employer. In an attempt to encourage high-value health behaviors to reduce the cost of healthcare benefits, many employers have adopted "wellness" programs to help incentivize employees to exercise, stop smoking, eat healthy, get checked for common risk factors and other behaviors that are known to be beneficial. App companies have also been working to do this for other payor populations, like Medicare or Medicaid.

The problem with the adoption by employer groups when it comes to thinking about the overall societal-level health system is that they are not the major drivers of cost. Medicare and Medicaid patient populations are still the sicker and more costly patients in the country, thus it is essential for innovations to also be focused and built to target these populations. But as a caveat, individuals in employer-based health insurance will eventually become eligible for Medicare, and thus their health behaviors during earlier years will impact their Medicare years.

As health behaviors serve as important risk factors for chronic illness, innovations that are able to effect meaningful and lasting improvement for individual choices and lifestyles will be important innovations in the fight for a healthier population. At the moment, everyone has an approach and a theory as to what types of programs will be effective. One of the beautiful things about innovation working on small, but important, problems from the patient level is that numerous approaches can be tried. Many will fail, but those that prove effective will gain traction as time progresses.

These failures are too often generalized to the entire space. As with any new technologies that gain "fad" status, critics will cite major failures of one promising innovation. But these failures teach us what works and what does not work, allowing for the next innovations to improve. The pursuit of innovation and better health systems will always achieve success as long as the goals and vision aim to produce benefits. Time is the only factor with these types of technologies. We will continue to innovate, iterate, and succeed in the pursuit of innovations that produce benefits.

Recently, Germany passed a law, the Digital Care Act, that will allow healthcare providers to prescribe digital therapeutics and apps for the purpose of improving medical care or treating a condition. These consumer/patient-facing technologies will continue to be developed, with the hope that self-management of conditions and health-impacting behaviors can be remotely modified for the better.

Prevention and proactive self-management are the ultimate goals of technologies like this, ones that use various techniques to accomplish a set of goals.

I have heard it said that the next great revolution has been theorized to be technology, but it will actually be behavioral sciences that can help people be better, more productive, and healthier versions of themselves.

Perhaps it will be behavioral science delivered via digital health technology.

## ASSISTIVE TECHNOLOGIES

With mobility impacting the ability of an older adult with a chronic illness to self-manage care, or, in the case of my mom, a younger patient who is very sick, there is interest in technologies that can help support patients in the home. In recent years, advances in battery capacity and size, as well as robotic technology, have garnered an interest in assistive technologies that can support older adults or patients in the home.

I was at a conference focused on the issues and trends in the longevity industry (as the market for technologies, products, and services for the aging US population has come to be known). That's where I learned about a company, backed by Amazon, called Labrador Systems.

The company is building assistive technologies and robots that can help patients take medications, manage daily living activities, and generally support people to stay in their homes longer when mobility becomes a challenge. These technologies can support patients in the home, and will become increasingly popular.

Mobility issues can effect an individual's ability to perform the activities of daily living and to self-manage the chronic conditions that commonly coincide with aging. Assistive technologies and robots that can support patients and older adults in the home are truly a vision of the future held by many, but one that will become a reality as the need for such innovations drives a revolution in research and development.

## HOME VISITS

It may come as a surprise, but the home visit has made a comeback. Harkening back to the origins of the American health system, physicians and nurses are increasingly finding themselves back in patients' homes. The ancient model of the community physician caring for sick patients in the home—such as that depicted by Luke Fildes in his 1891 painting, *The Doctor,* where a physician is compassionate and vigilant at the home bedside of an ill young girl—is now becoming more important to the American health system once more.

The return on investment for home visits can be very good. If it costs $400 for a nurse practitioner to visit a patient in the home and a few of those visits can help prevent a costly $30,000 hospitalization, then the upfront investment makes sense. Many organizations are beginning to explore these types of home-based and intensive services. The problem, though, is that the resources are not available to deliver these intensive services to all patients. This is where technologies can and are being used to augment and enhance a traditional model of care: the home visit.

Technologies are helping organizations decide which patients would most benefit from a home visit, as well as providing virtual home visits when an in-person visit is less necessary. Risk stratification of electronic health record data and claims data is being used to flag patients, tailor interventions for a higher likelihood of success, and to facilitate connections between medical provider and patient.

## ELEARNING

There has been a rapid development of electronic learning technologies in order to facilitate learning-at-scale for caregivers and patients. Self-management for conditions is complicated for those without a medical background and even for those with a medical background. Ensuring patients are able to confidently manage their own conditions is still the best and most resource-efficient means of helping patients maintain a positive health status for their condition. While this cannot be relied upon to solve the problem, it can still be helpful.

eLearning platforms are scalable technologies to help bridge that fifteen-minute clinician visit time. Explaining all the necessary components of self-management or warning signs for a chronic condition is not possible in fifteen-minutes of visit time. These digital platforms deliver effective content in patient-friendly ways to help extend the educational capacities of clinicians.

These technologies and their digital content are produced by experts in the field and augmented by experts in patient education and teachers. The adoption of these technologies has been slow because of reimbursement-related issues. Companies like Mytonomy and GetWellNetwork (started by a fellow Georgetown grad) produce educational content tailored to patients in order to help them understand their conditions, learn how to use medications, and to understand potential warning signs.

Mytonomy creates micro-learning videos that are short and engaging for inclusion in patient portals at hospitals. Instead of receiving hospital discharge instructions via a piece of paper, the hospital can assign videos to patients to provide more support in the form of engaging digital, visual content.

There are many companies trying to seize this space by developing content and online platforms to house the content. Regardless of the approach, the ability to bridge the time gap for physicians and nurses providing patient education is crucial. Advances in digital technology and content creation have enabled these companies to succeed at providing value to patients using a new medium. Healthcare is still very reliant on paper, but that is changing now that better means of communication are enabling improved patient engagement and education. The aim here is to support patients by helping them understand and support themselves.

This is the ultimate goal. Patients who can support and manage themselves are going to be more successful at managing their conditions. In this, the health system can facilitate this process, monitor patients remotely, and step in if there is a risk factor. Higher risk patients from the start can also receive higher intensity services and support as necessary.

* * *

Our time caring for my mom at home was challenging and uncertain. Fortunately, we knew when to ask for help and when something was going wrong. In high-risk patients, like my mom, conditions can change quickly and require rapid response. Supportive data collection, analysis, and monitoring by health professionals would have been very welcome to provide not only clinical support, but also peace of mind to both our family as caregivers and to my mom as a patient.

When she left the hospital, it was very scary. The confidence in the nurses and physicians to care for her should something go wrong was high in the hospital. At home, she was now with us most of the time. The stress and fear of something going wrong in the home was something we were forced to confront frequently.

Fortunately, innovations like RPM, telehealth, and eLearning are gaining adoption and will continue to provide benefits to patients and their families. Healthcare is moving into the home. These types of technologies will become the norm, as the payment environment incentivizes organizations to build programs incorporating these technologies and new models are put through clinical research validation.

## CHAPTER 23

# TECHNOLOGY THAT BREAKS DOWN BARRIERS

———

"We have to go back to the clinic tomorrow?" my mom asked with disappointment, after her lab values returned from the clinic late in the day, around 4 PM (we had arrived at 7:30 AM for an 8:00 AM appointment).

My mom sat in the infusion chair or her wheelchair all day long, received infusions of blood products, and by now was very tired. But we would have to get up again at 6:30 AM to get my mom up, dressed, and into the car for another long, taxing trip to the clinic. Time after time, this same process would occur.

She was prescribed new medications and new appointments were made to also see her cardiologist to monitor the progress of her heart. We continued to travel even further away to see her eye surgeon for her continued struggle with vision loss due to infection.

The new medications required a stop at the pharmacy or a whole new trip. The new appointments required bringing new medication lists to share with the other specialists, and often required two caregivers (most likely my seventy-year-old grandma and myself) to move and transport my mom to these appointments due to her inability to walk without a walker or wheelchair.

We, as caregivers, were tired emotionally and physically. My mom was dealing with her physical condition, the emotional toll of it, and the challenges of navigating a healthcare system designed for the system and not the very sick patient.

But we were all determined to beat this disease and to overcome any challenges that were presented; there were many. During this time though, I could not help but wonder what happened to people who were far less fortunate, had little help from family, and were less educated on both the care of a patient's medical condition and in general.

We were flying blind during our first experience caring for a patient with leukemia, congestive heart failure, infection, and eye surgery. We had little experience with many of the tasks necessary during care, and were unsure when to be concerned about things. Thankfully, I knew where to go for reliable information, have excellent reading comprehension skills, and understand medical terminology. But most patients in this country are not able to do this, and thus being sent home with a very sick patient presents a major barrier to successful home-based management of conditions.

The constant need for transport to appointments, the lack of services coordination, the need to make multiple trips to the pharmacy, the inexperience, and the uncertainty were major barriers. We had good commercial insurance coverage and more resources than many American families, but financial barriers add up on top of the barriers of transportation, health literacy, education, time, and uncertainty faced by thousands of other American families.

What about the patients on Medicaid? The poor patients? What about elderly patients and people who faced this journey alone and without help or the ability to truly grasp what they were told by their healthcare providers? Barriers to providing care to our sickest patients are numerous and contribute to the failure of our health system in terms of cost and quality. The ones who are unable to understand medication interactions, who cannot afford their medications, or do not have reliable transportation: what do they do?

When patients are discharged from the hospital or leave a clinic appointment, they are more or less left to their own devices. With so much healthcare experienced and required outside of facilities and by individuals with little support, the system fails to solve patient needs that are directly related to the outcomes of the services provided.

Solving for patient barriers to successful care and self-management is necessary in order to make progress toward a health system that is more universally effective and cost-efficient.

* * *

In addition to collecting data, exchanging stored information, and performing analysis for other purposes, new technologies also have the ability to facilitate the removal or mitigation of patient barriers to care.

Patients with fewer resources have an even more difficult time navigating and managing their own care and health. This is a major problem that costs billions, and leads to bad outcomes in terms of quality of care and quality of life. If we want to reduce costs and improve quality, addressing these barriers is crucial.

We know that medication adherence is one of the many problems that drive these bad outcomes, and part of the reason for poor medication adherence is simply forgetting, while other reasons include prohibitive cost, transportation, and a distrust of the medical establishment brought on by historical discrimination.[37]

This is one of the many barriers faced by patients when diagnosed and treated for their conditions. Lack of transportation to pick up medications and to attend appointments is another barrier. Inability to understand instructions due to poor literacy and lack of education is also a big barrier. Obvious cost barriers exist, as health services are expensive and even more expensive without health coverage. A lack of

---

37  M Brown, Marie T., Jennifer Bussell, Suparna Dutta, Katherine Davis, Shelby Strong, and Suja Mathew. 2016. "Medication Adherence: Truth and Consequences." *American Journal of the Medical Sciences* 351 (4): 387–99.

caregivers because family have to work to pay their own bills, or no family existing nearby are other big barriers once the patient gets home, just as is the inability to pay for a full- or part-time professional caregiver.

For this population plagued by age and socioeconomic factors and driven by poverty and discrimination, scalable and affordable technology can be used to reduce the many barriers to services and self-management that exist throughout the healthcare system.

Besides monitoring clinical data to better match patients to diagnoses and interventions proactively, or to monitor at more frequent intervals, the removal of barriers is also something to be facilitated by technologies.

\* \* \*

It has long been rumored that Amazon is looking to disrupt the healthcare industry through some serious innovation, backed by tons of capital and plenty of access to potential customers.

In May 2019, Christina Farr, a technology and health reporter with CNBC, wrote the following about a move that indicated Amazon's anticipated entry into the healthcare industry:

*"It was May 2018, and PillPack CEO TJ Parker was in Seattle to meet with a small contingent from Amazon.*

*Suitors had been swarming around his online pharmacy, which was taking on CVS and Walgreens and growing rapidly in the process. Walmart was deep in talks with the Boston-based start-up, and pharmaceutical maker Novartis was also hovering. But bankers from Frank Quattrone's Qatalyst Partners suggested that Parker and co-founder and product chief Elliot Cohen fly across country for a meeting with one particular Amazon executive: Nader Kabbani. A fourteen-year company veteran and guest concert pianist with the Seattle Symphony who'd recently been named Amazon's vice president of consumables, Kabbani shared Parker's concern about the pharmacy industry and the dominant players' inability or unwillingness to put the consumer first."*

TJ Parker and PillPack were already succeeding at being the Amazon of pharmacy. They were creating personalized, easy to use, and shipped medication regimens to customers. Amazon's subsequent $753 million acquisition of PillPack sent waves across the industry, and, in particular, it led to a massive hit to the dominant retail pharmacy players; they watched their stock prices drop.

Amazon has been in the business of solving problems for consumers for many years at this point, and had set its sights on some big problems in healthcare—the nation's largest industry.

The problem identified, and of interest to Amazon as indicated by the PillPack acquisition, is medication adherence and the barriers associated with a brick-and-mortar-based medication distribution system. Barriers for some, inconvenient for others, but nevertheless a big problem.

While Amazon's interest in the space probably has more to do with making the service available to its millions of Amazon

Prime customers to add additional value (while also winning their pharmacy business); the effect of shipping medications to patients in a well-designed package that helps them organize and manage their medications is still, at its most basic, to reduce barriers to medication access.

Mail-order pharmacies have been operating for many years by now, and we know that it is much easier and more guaranteed that a patient receives their medication if it is shipped to their front door. These pharmacies often are used to ship patients' medications for the treatment of chronic conditions because they take them on a regular schedule and require them on a long-term basis. Amazon is making this existing model more patient-centric, and is leveraging its existing distribution and shipping channels to win business from its vast captive audience.

Shipping medications to patients is not the most innovative concept because it has been around for a while, but moving into this business will allow Amazon to set its disruption engine to work on data collected through this process and through its additional products. Namely, Alexa voice-technologies.

In addition to the existing PillPack model, Amazon's new pharmacy customers will be able to receive medication reminders via their in-home Alexa voice assistant, track their deliveries, and refill their prescriptions. All of this will be accomplished by simply speaking to Alexa.

Now, people will receive medication reminders in their home via the Alexa system, will have those medications shipped to their home—packaged in a user-friendly manner, and refilled easily. This is such a simple innovation that can impact the ways in which people receive care and manage their medications.

Thus, barriers can be reduced, and, through partnerships with Medicaid programs, managed care health plans, and other organizations, these technologies can be offered to high-risk populations. For seniors, in particular, voice-based technology also reduces the barrier to using technology on a mobile device, and helps facilitate external processes in the home thus reducing even more barriers.

Voice-based technologies such as Amazon's Alexa and Google's Home products are going to be major game changers because of their ease of use, passive data collection capabilities, and location in the home. These technologies are accessible by all and inexpensive to deliver—the perfect recipe for success.

Several organizations have begun using Alexa's voice technology for important healthcare applications. Organizations like the Boston Children's Hospital are using Alexa to help monitor patients after surgery. The application, called MyChildren's Enhanced Recovery After Surgery Alexa skill, allows for remote check-ins after discharge.

According to Boston Children's Hospital in a statement:

*It allows parents and caregivers to conduct remote check-ins through Alexa, providing care teams with updates on their child's recovery progress, including activity level, appetite, and*

*pain management. Parents and caregivers can also use the skill
to access information regarding the child's upcoming post-op
appointments. Simply say, "Alexa, open My Children's" to get
started.* [38]

Voice technology has tremendous applications across the
healthcare industry due to accessibility, scalability, afford-
ability, and the potential effectiveness of home-based data
collection and patient engagement.

Transportation barriers like getting to the pharmacy or
appointments, financial barriers to care, health literacy issues
driven by low education or general difficulty understanding
medical terminology, racial bias, and other major barriers to
successful care are being attacked by innovators through the
use of technologies for the reasons mentioned above.

Companies and innovators that can address patient-level
barriers in an effective manner, inexpensively, and at scale
will be successful. Besides Amazon's shipping and technology, companies like Lyft are also getting into healthcare. As
a scalable, easy to use, and up-and-running company, Lyft
has tremendous benefits for healthcare organizations.

In an attempt to reduce transportation barriers and by taking
advantage of state and federal policies (non-emergency medical transportation programs [NEMT])trying to enhance
patient access to health services through transportation, Lyft
has created a health division within their popular ride-hail-
ing service. Lyft Health partners with hospitals, Medicaid

---

38   Boston Children's Hospital

insurers, and other organizations to help patients find transportation to their appointments. The scalable, mobile, and inexpensive solution provides an excellent benefit to healthcare organizations and patients.

Rather than a hospital system having to buy its own vans, cars, or contracting with an ambulance company to provide all non-emergent medical transport, Lyft provides a quick and ready solution to help solve patient access barriers in an efficient manner, right from the patient's mobile device. Now, a patient can hail a Lyft driver from their phone in order to get to their medical appointment that is subsidized or free.

Reducing the transportation barrier or lack of financial ability to afford transportation, Lyft Health is helping low-income patients make it to their healthcare appointments—thus solving a major barrier for a group of patients who are often at higher risk for chronic illness or exacerbation of existing chronic illness.

Sometimes brick and mortar appointments are necessary for procedures, but home-based and mobile technologies can also impact transportation-related issues.

* * *

Companies and innovators are using technology to bridge the gap between patient and healthcare system to make healthcare more accessible, effective, and efficient. In order to better tailor diagnoses and treatments to patients from better use of data, new data collection, and predictive analytics, patients must first be able to meet the health system.

I mentioned that the issues associated with large-scale-only healthcare system reform efforts lack the pointedness to reach patients and to improve universal effectiveness of healthcare delivery systems at the point where patient meets health services. These reform efforts are always centered around improving coverage from insurance and extending coverage to those without access to it.

These efforts *are* important, and help by breaking down financial barriers to care and access to important preventive services. But they are not the way to fundamentally improve US healthcare in and of themselves, as they are often touted.

Medicare-for-All and the ACA are important movements to improve healthcare coverage. But once coverage is obtained, the system is not effective enough to produce the desired outcomes—that is, a healthier population. Unfortunately, champions of healthcare reform are caught up on coverage because that basic level of requirement has not yet been met due to political and ideological reasons.

To those working on coverage improvements and research, I say keep up the good work. But my focus in this book is on innovations that, once coverage is obtained, drive better outcomes in terms of models of health service delivery. Simply having coverage does not guarantee success. In fact, we know that sometimes *more* healthcare services under the current model can actually be detrimental to health.

The work of researchers like Dr. Elliott Fisher at Dartmouth shows that healthcare services across the country are heterogeneous in their effectiveness and utilization, and that sometimes more healthcare is worse. The bottom line is that the current model of institution, reactive, and episodic healthcare delivery does not produce sufficient results toward improving the health and wellness of the country.

Innovations that address barriers to care and support new delivery models that focus on proactive services rather than reactive services are necessary to drive major improvements in outcomes and a reduction in overall demand for health services due to a healthier underlying population.

# CHAPTER 24

# THE FUTURE IS
# DIFFERENT

---

We know that the US healthcare system is deeply flawed. Patients struggle to navigate their care journeys. Bills pile up or deter people from seeking care in the first place. In many cases, patients receive services that provide little value. The system as a whole is worse than comparable countries, with worse outcomes at the population level, and has higher rates of preventable hospitalizations.

We know that healthcare services vary in effectiveness. Different facilities have different issues. Health insurance is difficult to navigate and understand. Patients have numerous barriers to successful treatment. Our models of matching patients with services are flawed and produce poor outcomes at large. Our system fails to support patients outside the four walls of the healthcare facilities, data is used poorly, technology adoption has been slow, and *we know that the system is not built to drive health and wellness.*

Again, chronic illnesses like diabetes, heart disease, cancer, and COPD drive most of the spending and are poorly managed. We know that about 75 percent of healthcare's trillions of dollars are spent on care for chronic conditions. These conditions are life-long afflictions developed due to behaviors and risk factors, then exacerbated because of the same poor health system clinical management. The cost produced by these conditions comes largely from poor management and subsequent costly services, such as emergency department visits and hospitalizations.

We know that the healthcare delivery system waits for something to go wrong and then steps in once that has already happened. It's an episodic and reactive model. At the same time, this system is reinforced because more patients requiring more services lead to more revenue for healthcare organizations delivering care because of fee-for-service payment models.

The majority of the national discussion about healthcare reform or efforts to solve these problems involves large sweeping legislation looking to change and extend more insurance coverage. This is without recognition that both fee-for-service incentives and existing delivery models are insufficient to improve the health of patients with chronic illness—though, admittedly, are a necessary pre-condition.

While coverage extension is a good thing, is a necessary precursor to delivery model reform helping patients, and is a noble pursuit, the underlying delivery system and patient-level problems require innovation. Relying on coverage improvements to solve national quality and cost issues alone is not enough.

Far too often, those looking to go a step further than coverage-only reform cite price regulation and care rationing as the methods by which cost can be decreased. But there is a third option that is much more difficult, but actually aligns with the goals of a healthcare system—to produce societal wellness. That third option is to reduce the demand for healthcare services by actually improving the health of the population.

The health system is not very good at this type of reform and has been inhibited in trying more aggressive strategies by fee-for-service incentives. But now, with increasing adoption of alternative payment models like ACOs, there exists a never-before-seen opportunity to experiment with new models of care payment and delivery.

Value-based payment models like the ACO have now aligned incentives between patient, provider, and payor to accelerate adoption of new models. These changes are located at the point where the patient meets the healthcare system, and are now enabling the first steps toward more supportive and proactive models.

ACOs and similar organizations are exploring new models and programs that can enable them to improve patient condition management in order to prevent utilization of costly healthcare service. This has been the greatest challenge of the ACO model and has led to failure by some ACOs to meet the goals of the payment model. But there have been marked successes and overall, I believe that the model is effective due to scientific studies and program evaluations looking at outcomes.

ACOs are still in their early stages, but those achieving successes through new models of care coordination, advanced analytics, and better use of previously unused information are continuing to enroll more and more patients. As with any new innovation, there is a learning curve necessary to achieve success and, in this case, the healthcare system is now learning how to provide services in a manner that can help patients remain healthy and in their homes.

To achieve greater successes and to continue achieving success, ACOs have begun adopting new digital health technologies to gain insights into their patient populations, to identify opportunities impacting positive health improvement, and to break down barriers to care. Digital health technologies will enable the health system to collect, exchange, and analyze patient data in order to better diagnose and tailor interventions to patients.

Through digital solutions, the health system is now able to extend its data collection reach, improve its efficiency through automation of previously manual processes, and develop new insights through advanced analytics. With these new capabilities, digital tools can enable the health system to extend a supportive reach into the home to support and monitor patients outside the four walls of the healthcare organization. Communication on-demand and real-time, proactive service models are being developed to fundamentally flip the way the healthcare delivery system works when caring for patients with chronic illness.

Digital tools like mobile devices such as the iPhone and other smartphones, wearables like the Apple Watch, Fitbit, or CarePredict's proprietary device, improved electronic health records, IoT-enabled diagnostic tools (like blood glucose meters, blood pressure cuffs, voice-technology, and video conferencing tools) are poised to drive innovation in healthcare services like never before.

These tools and incentives are being used by innovators, researchers, and companies to break down patient barriers to care and to enhance the connection of the patient to medical knowledge. Truly, as health service delivery models and patient tools are made to reflect the needs and problems faced by patients, the outcomes will follow. Patients experience health and their health journey in a way that is currently out of alignment with the current system designed to care for them.

The discovery of patient needs with user-centered design thinking, combined with the acceleration of technology, and new incentives aimed at changing the system's interaction with the patient are the primers for the future of the healthcare system. We are standing at the beginning of a revolution in not only biomedical science but the system's ability to deliver the promises of medicine to the patients who need them.

\* \* \*

The healthcare system of the future is proactive, enabled by mobile technology, and informed by actionable data. It is a partnership between technology, policy, and frontline clinical professionals.

Data is, of course, prioritized. New types of data are collected and combined with existing data sets. The data is used for research and real-time analytics to determine important information about the patient's condition and risk for certain future developments.

Medical and public health knowledge and research are made actionable through service delivery models that act on the real-time data collected from patients who are using wearables, who use home-based lab tests, and who self-report important information into their mobile devices.

In the background, clinical and claims data along with new data are monitored by automated algorithms and analytics tools to flag patients who are at risk of an adverse event, bad outcome, or emergency department visit. When flagged, a healthcare professional is able to reach out to that patient to intervene with a recommendation made by the analytics and based on a comparison across thousands of similar patient journeys to predict effectiveness.

Patient barriers to treatment and care are identified via questionnaires or through previously unlinked financial, educational, and other social data sets to understand how to best support and enable that patient to navigate and obtain health services.

High-risk patients like my mom are able to receive more intensive services and support because we know they are high risk, so early investments and better tools can lead to better outcomes that generate cost savings.

These patients with multiple chronic illnesses are seeing multiple providers who have access to all their medical records, test results, and medication lists, as well as all other relevant information. Providers are all alerted about potentially dangerous interactions in new prescriptions, they are alerted about the patient's risk, and are able to coordinate their efforts to best match the patient's needs and experiences.

In a similar vein, clinicians of the future practice interdisciplinary collaboration as they know that patients experience health all at once, as opposed to independently and in a fragmented manner as the system exists currently. Driven by data and enabled by information technology, clinicians can collaborate across disciplines to leverage expertise across the globe—unlocking tremendous collective knowledge.

Across disciplines, the traditional silos between specialists, primary care, and mental health providers are demolished due to the new and increased ability to seamlessly collaborate for their patients. Fueled by payment reform that aligns incentives with digital technology, a patient's health is viewed not as separate physical and mental but as a continuous experience by that individual. The role that both mental health and physical health play in an individual's wellbeing is known, and models of care reflect that knowledge.

Physicians and other clinical staff can collect patient data in the home to reduce the need for office visits and transportation. If a patient is flagged at-risk for something, a clinician can set up a telehealth video call in order to discuss with the patient, ask questions, and make alterations to the patient's treatment plan.

Through changes to attribution and responsibility for patients such as those under ACO models, health can be viewed as a long-term investment where certain treatments, procedures, and programs used now will be known to impact future healthcare status and service utilization. Instead of the reactive and short-term mindset we have now, patient health will be viewed as an investment that can be made due to the assembly of longitudinal health journey records that can allow for the determination of the interventions that produce long-term value (see Komodo Health).

Healthcare professionals of the future recognize that there are finite resources, meaning that high-value services are necessary to have an efficient system. Analytics and clinical decision tools help physicians and other professionals decide which interventions will produce the most value for a patient. With data-driven decision support, clinicians have the ability to lay out options and risks for patients to guide their decisions over their own care journey.

Health and wellness is a lifelong pursuit and patients have their own heterogenous needs when it comes to managing and maintaining a positive health status. The health system recognizes this and has built models of care that identify these individual needs, and in turn tailor interventions to patients more effectively and automatically due to the use of technologies.

The health system, policymakers, and frontline clinicians know that biomedical treatments may not be the complete answer for everyone. They know that living a healthy lifestyle with a balanced diet and exercise helps to mitigate risk factors for chronic disease, and they use technology to help proactively support their patients in their pursuit of better health behaviors.

The system acknowledges that socioeconomic factors impact a patient's risk for the development of a chronic illness or the risk of exacerbation of an existing one, and they have developed models that help connect patients to housing, food, and the other basic needs before expecting the patient to achieve adequate health. The system is able to support these patients with inexpensive digital and mobile technologies to provide care in the home, or homeless shelter, when transportation and location make travel to medical facilities difficult.

Healthcare professionals of the future are fierce advocates at the societal level for social programs that help low-income individuals and older adults maintain positive health and wellbeing by addressing societal level risk factors for disease like racism, violence, poverty, social isolation, and environmental factors. While these goals are set at a high bar, healthcare professionals understand the practical importance and effects of these societal issues that directly affect the health of this nation's population and therefore its economic wellbeing.

All of this is made possible because of the intersection between new payment models that alter and align incentives and the acceleration of digital health technology and its application to patient-level problems. The health system of the future is not perfect, but it has unlocked data to continue learning how to continuously, proactively improve toward a society with greatly improved health and wellness.

## CHAPTER 25

# INNOVATING FOR THE FUTURE

———

I stopped at a garage sale on my way to the hospital one morning in early July after my mom was readmitted—the clinic found her with a low-grade fever. A fever, for leukemia patients, is a big warning sign that merits readmission to the Bone Marrow Transplant unit. After roughly two months at home and under outpatient care, she was back in the hospital.

As caregivers, this felt like both a setback and an unfortunate relief. For my mom, being back in the hospital was a big disappointment and a blow to progress. While we were also disappointed and did not want to see her distressed, the stress of caregiving and managing her care at home was alleviated because she was back in professional hands. At this point, we felt like a few hospitalizations would be normal as her condition seemed to be improving overall and an extra set of eyes to collect more data on her condition could be beneficial.

We fell back into the old routine where we would alternate time at the hospital to keep my mom company. So, I would make the all-too-familiar drive back and forth between the hospital and our home to sit with my mom as she lay in a new room on the same hospital floor in which we spent months before.

For two weeks, we went through this routine; we were expecting a faster discharge after the fever was reduced and her condition stabilized.

After getting back in my car, once I perused the garage sale to take my mind off the present situation for a moment, my phone started ringing.

"Hello?"

"Robert, are you on your way to the hospital?" my dad asked.

"Yes, I'll be there in five minutes."

"Okay, we are all here already, and we are meeting with the doctor."

I was surprised by this news because I thought I was the only one going to the hospital that day. As I drove, the sinking feeling once again returned—I could only imagine what was to be discussed during the meeting with the physician. Anything outside the normal fifteen-minute or less visit was cause for concern.

I arrived and found my whole family sitting in the dark room with my mom, in a surprisingly clear mind, sitting up in the bed.

"Son, your mom has decided to stop treatment and go home. The doctor called me this morning and made the recommendation due to the apparent ineffectiveness of the new leukemia drug for her condition. We are going to transfer her to hospice care at home," my dad said to me in a low voice as I entered the room, clothed in my perfectly positioned protective gown, hands washed, and hopeful.

The room was dark and quiet, filled with tissues, as we all surrounded my mom. My sister, just informed, was laying with her head down on the couch at the other end of the room. I took a seat in the plastic chair directly across from the hospital bed. In shock, I sat there as we all waited for her hematologist-oncologist to enter the room.

The hallway light from the small window on the hospital room door was the only light shining into the room. I sat— crushed, tired, and with long held-back tears streaming down my face, recognizing the shock I was experiencing as I retreated into my own head.

The door opened as her physician and nurse entered, light shining around them in their long white coats. On this hospital floor, as mediators of life and death, those white-coated clinicians have seen this process far too many times.

"Are you ready to go home?" he said to my mom.

"Yes."

"We will try and get you out of here and back home by the end of the day."

With that, he and the others left the room to arrange for an ambulance to take her back to our house.

All I could do was watch as all the efforts to ensure my mom's chances of surviving this disease over the past six months were unable to prevent this moment. Among sadness, disbelief, and shock, I felt a sense of failure. I questioned all of our actions. I toiled over the idea that there was something else that could have been done.

I sat on the hospital bed with my mom, as we all began to understand what this meant.

\* \* \*

We lost my mom to her conditions on July 16th. The CML, the chemotherapy, the hospital, the long drives, and the sixteen-plus medications took their toll on her. She passed away in hospice care at our home. She died in her own bed and on her own terms.

I remember that it was an incredibly hot day and I remember where I was, but I do not recall much else. My mind, in an attempt to protect me from the sheer shock of the event, has blocked out much of the days afterward. There were no more visits to the clinic. There was no more contact with her physicians. There was no more contact with the nurses who had become our friends. There were no more test results waiting to come in, no more goal of getting healthy enough for a bone marrow transplant in pursuit of a cure. It was all over, just like that.

That worn pink binder sat, unopened, on the table next to the large plastic bin of medications and the blood pressure cuffs and the stethoscopes and the hundreds of papers and bills.

There was no manual for how to move on after the loss or the events of the six months prior. The hospice agency left a small pamphlet titled *Gone from my Sight*. The health system took us in, tossed us around, and dropped us out as quickly as we fell into it. After all of the interactions, struggles, appointments, and prescriptions, we had a house full of medical equipment, a box full of hundreds of thousands of dollars' worth of pills representing billions of dollars in medical research, and a small pamphlet.

My mom's condition was deadly, complicated by co-morbidities, and challenging to overcome from the start. But despite this, she and we tried. We gave it our best shot fueled by hope and science. But in the end, the medicine failed to succeed.

My professional friend, and one-summer mentor, Dr. Clarence Davis M.D., Chief Medical Officer of Wellcare Health Plans of Georgia, likes to remind everyone that "in medicine sometimes there are just bad outcomes" regardless of the quality of services provided.

Sometimes better, more efficient care might not result in the desired outcome. This is one of the fundamental challenges of healthcare.

\* \* \*

In the years after that day, I struggled to accept and understand what happened. To some extent, I still do. I returned to school and continued to focus on studying the very system that caused so much struggle during a time where we had looked to it for hope and support. In the year after, I was unable to do much more than study and try to keep moving forward.

During this period, I spent a good deal of time searching and yearning for the day I could look back on it all from a new perspective. I knew that one day I would feel like I had overcome and accepted the trauma of it all. I knew that there would be a "reunion-show-esque moment" where I could view the whole thing from a different place and say, "Wow, that was a lot to handle."

Now, several more years later, I have realized "that day" will never come from looking back at what happened. The memories and stories will always be present, and we will all carry them with us for the rest of our lives. Rather, it will only come from looking forward, searching for and building something better.

\* \* \*

My mom was a tremendous person. Like all moms, I am sure, she carried her love for her family and children up to the last moments of her life. She was an excellent student, obtaining three degrees from three universities. She was an excellent teacher, with many of her former students traveling to make it to her funeral and many more sharing stories of how she impacted their lives from the fifth grade onward. She was never one to seek recognition for her accomplishments or the lengths she would go to for her students.

She was a roll-up her sleeves, get the job done kind of person. But not the boring kind, one who knew how to have fun. Despite a cancer diagnosis eight years prior to her death, she continued teaching the next generation in school and at home. Not only in school subjects but about living life to the fullest, perseverance, and grit. A condition that has brought many to their knees drove her to experience and accomplish more in the face of uncertainty.

In the years of life before her death, she would complete a Tough Mudder 10K run complete with electric shocks, run several half marathons, raise two children and get them sent off to college, complete a specialist degree in education, volunteer at and lead fundraisers, teach hundreds of students, become Teacher of the Year, ensure I knew that she was the only Valentine I ever really needed and that I cleaned my bathroom, and added a good deal of needed spontaneity to our lives.

She was a fighter, and, despite a role reversal during her care journey, she maintained her role as my Mom right up to the end.

During one of our final conversations, and in a rare moment of mental clarity toward the end, she made clear her intention that her death became a motivation for me above anything else. In traditional fashion, she made it clear that she would have it no other way.

One of the few items I have of hers is a sign that sat in her classroom. It reads, *I'm not bossy, I just know what you should be doing.* It sits atop my dresser as a constant reminder of my mom.

Since the day she died in mid-July, everything, for better or worse, has been framed by this experience, including writing this book. My initial pursuit of medicine and a healthcare profession was driven by other reasons, but it changed. It became personal.

\* \* \*

Health issues and impactful health system experiences are ubiquitous. If you talk to enough people who work in healthcare, you are likely to find a story. After a bit of discussion and some personal sharing, many people have a story that drives their work and passion for the pursuit of something better.

From the tech start-up founders like Jerry Wilmink at CarePredict, physicians and nurses who learn new stories each day, to the researchers like Dr. Elliott Fisher who have dedicated their lives to rejecting the status quo and the relentless pursuit of better health for all—everyone has a story.

The combination of academic aptitude, a passion for learning, outside-the-box thinking, and a deeply personal mission is a powerful recipe to disrupt and reform one of the world's most important industries.

Innovation is never easy. New ideas and technologies are rejected by many to be pursued by the few who *know* that there are always better ways to do things. Many of the innovations I have explored in this book are believed by many to be short-lived fads or even outright failures. Many ACOs have failed to achieve the goals of the program, but many have also proven successful. Many digital health companies have failed to achieve outcomes or adoption, but a number, like CarePredict, have been successful.

It is easy to discount innovations during the research and development cycle and in failures. But it is much harder to learn from mistakes, accept failure, and to try again. The future belongs to those with the audacity to keep trying for better, despite critics. If innovation was easy, then we would live in a utopia. But it is the hardest thing to do.

And, in the case of healthcare, it is the right thing to do. There is no better pursuit than that which elevates the health, wellness, and happiness of our societies. In the end, there is little else that matters than the time we have to experience life with those closest to us.

The next generation of healthcare researchers, managers, and providers will continue to build upon the work of those leaders who came before them. Leaders and innovators like Dr. Elliott Fisher, Jerry Wilmink, and Taylor Justice have paved the way to a better healthcare future by thinking outside the box and trying to fundamentally change the system for better by innovating in ways that bring better healthcare to the patient.

They set out to achieve something better for us all, and their work will continue to effect the lives of millions of patients.

It is not through the same old strategies and attempts that healthcare will become better, safer, more effective, more equitable, and less expensive. It is through taking the risk to look differently at the patient experience, to think differently from the ways things are currently done, to believe there can be a better way, and to enact the consistent pursuit of good.

Healthcare is an industry like no other. It is complex, highly esoteric, and driven by scientific principles. But above all, it is an expression of our humanity—it is a noble pursuit to promote public health. Every day, I see people driven by a deep desire to do good in the healthcare industry. Standing on the shoulders of those who desired the same before them, today's students, entrepreneurs, young professionals, physicians, and academics are looking to push the boundaries of the industry, to break down barriers, and to work between disciplines and more collaboratively than ever before.

The next generation grew up in the digital world where information exchange, mobile engagement, and technology is second nature. There is hope for a health system where new ways of thinking, payment models, and digital health technology coexist to improve the delivery of medical knowledge to the patients who need them in an efficient, effective, and equitable manner.

Improving the delivery of healthcare services to our nation's sickest, poorest, and most at-risk individuals is not only a good economic investment, but is also the right thing to do for a happier, healthier, and more balanced society.

We should all feel hope—despite our current challenges—knowing that where there is great suffering, need, and opportunity there will always be people willing to speak up and act and to try something new. The healthcare industrial complex is immense, the organizational inertias are strong, and the patient is the one to bite the bullet.

But in healthcare, there will always be those fueled by deep-seated personal stories or a desire to have a positive impact that will lead them to relentlessly pursue, in the face of tremendous opposition, *innovation for wellness.*

# APPENDIX

---

## CHAPTER 1:

- Aspril, Joshua, and JH Bloomberg School of Public Health. "US Healthcare Spending Highest Among Developed Countries." Johns Hopkins Bloomberg School of Public Health, January 8, 2019.

- Anderson, Gerard F, Uwe E Reinhardt, Peter S Hussey, and Varduhi Petrosyan. 2003. "It's The Prices, Stupid: Why The United States Is So Different From Other Countries." Health Affairs 22 (3): 89–105.

- *Anderson, Gerard F., Peter Hussey, and Varduhi Petrosyan. "It's Still The Prices, Stupid: Why The US Spends So Much On Healthcare, And A Tribute To Uwe Reinhardt." Health Affairs 38, no. 1 (2019): 87–95.*

- Dzau, Victor J., Mark B. McClellan, J. Michael McGinnis, Sheila P. Burke, Molly J. Coye, Angela Diaz, Thomas A. Daschle, et al. 2017. "Vital Directions for Health and Healthcare." *Jama* 317 (14): 1461.

## CHAPTER 2:

- Anderson, Gerard F., Peter Hussey, and Varduhi Petrosyan. *"It's Still The Prices, Stupid: Why The US Spends So Much On Healthcare, And A Tribute To Uwe Reinhardt." Health Affairs 38, no. 1 (2019): 87–95.*

- See the exchanges at healthcare.gov

- Berchick, Edward R., Emily Hood, and Jessica C. Barnett, Current Population Reports, P60-264, Health Insurance Coverage in the United States: 2017, US Government Printing Office, Washington, DC, 2018

- Buchmueller, Thomas C.; Monheit, Alan C. (2009). "Employer-Sponsored Health Insurance and the Promise of Health Insurance Reform". *Inquiry.* **46** (2): 187–202.

## CHAPTER 3:

- Sambamoorthi, Usha, Xi Tan, and Arijita Deb. 2015. "Multiple Chronic Conditions and Healthcare Costs among Adults." *Expert Review of Pharmacoeconomics and Outcomes Research* 15 (5): 823–32.

- Castaño, Adam, and Mathew S Maurer. 2015. "Multiple Chronic Conditions and Labor Force Outcomes: A Population Study of US Adults." *American Journal of Medicine* 20 (2): 163–78.

- Harris, L. Jeff, Ilana Graetz, Pradeep S.B. Podila, Jim Wan, Teresa M. Waters, and James E. Bailey. 2016. "Characteristics of Hospital and Emergency Care Super-Utilizers with Multiple

Chronic Conditions." *Journal of Emergency Medicine* 50 (4): e203–14.

- Adams, Mary L., Joseph Grandpre, David L. Katz, and Douglas Shenson. 2019. "The Impact of Key Modifiable Risk Factors on Leading Chronic Conditions." *Preventive Medicine* 120 (June 2018)

- Cockerham, William C., Bryant W. Hamby, and Gabriela R. Oates. 2017. "The Social Determinants of Chronic Disease." *American Journal of Preventive Medicine* 52 (1): S5–12.

## CHAPTER 4:
- "The World's Most Valuable Resource Is No Longer Oil, but Data." The Economist. The Economist Newspaper.

- World Health Organization. (2004). ICD-10 : international statistical classification of diseases and related health problems : tenth revision, 2nd ed. World Health Organization.

## CHAPTER 6:
- *"Leukemia - Chronic Myeloid - CML: Statistics | Cancer.Net". Archived from the original on 12 November 2014.*

## CHAPTER 10:
- Agency for Healthcare Research and Quality, Healthcare Cost and Utilization Project, State Inpatient Databases disparities analytic file, 2009

- Wammes, Joost Johan Godert, Philip J. van der Wees, Marit A.C. Tanke, Gert P. Westert, and Patrick P.T. Jeurissen. 2018. "Systematic Review of High-Cost Patients' Characteristics and Healthcare Utilisation." *BMJ Open* 8 (9): e023113.


## CHAPTER 13:
- American College of Physicians


## CHAPTER 14:
- Longyear, Robert L. 2019. "Medicaid ACOs, Information Systems, and Transitioning from Reactive to Proactive Care." *Georgetown University Repository.*

- Impact of Accountable Care Organizations on Utilization, Care, and Outcomes: A Systematic Review. Kaufman. 2019.


## CHAPTER 16:
- Cockerham, William C, Bryant W Hamby, and Gabriela R Oates. 2014. "The Social Determinants of Chronic Disease." *Am J Prev Med* 52: 1–14.

- Motivation and personality. New York: Harper and Row. **Maslow**, A. H. (1987)


## CHAPTER 17:
- "Technology." *Merriam-Webster.com.* 2011. https://www.merriam-webster.com (8 May 2011)

## CHAPTER 22:

- *American Heart Association*

- *Centers for Medicare and Medicaid Services. "Chronic conditions among Medicare beneficiaries, chartbook, 2012 edition." Baltimore, MD 11 (2012): 15-21*

- Deloitte 2018 Survey of US Physicians

- Vivify Health Case Studies

- *Vivify Health: UPMC and Vivify - Improving Care Through Remote Patient Monitoring*

## CHAPTER 23:

- M Brown, Marie T., Jennifer Bussell, Suparna Dutta, Katherine Davis, Shelby Strong, and Suja Mathew. 2016. "Medication Adherence: Truth and Consequences." *American Journal of the Medical Sciences* 351 (4): 387–99.

- Boston Children's Hospital

Made in the USA
Columbia, SC
15 April 2020